On *The Long Way Home: Detours and Discoveries*

Tom Montgomery Fate's masterful literary journeys—aptly named "detours of intention"—remind me of why the essay is such an engaging and powerful form. *The Long Way Home* is a deeply felt and beautifully written exploration of the search to find home, both in the landscape and in ourselves.
—Michael P. Branch, author, *On the Trail of the Jackalope*

Tom Fate is a refreshingly self-critical pilgrim, and is bent on traveling to the most honest place in his heart, and we follow too, as he mourns and connects.
—S.L. Wisenberg, author, *Holocaust Girls*

In the tradition of May Sarton's *Journal of Solitude*, Tom Fate takes the reader on an interior exploration through exterior landscapes. Monks, canoes, and travels abroad reveal the roving mind of Fate as he not only lives his life, but creates a life of meaning.
—Taylor Brorby, author, *Boys and Oil*

Tom Montgomery Fate's essays are thoughtful, beautifully written wanderings into landscapes of family, faith, and diverse places traveled over the arc of an adventurous and well-examined life. Like any wise traveler, Fate knows it's the journey, not the destination, that matters—and that wherever we're from never leaves our hearts.
—Cassie Kircher, author, *Farflung*

Tom Fate writes with the gift of compassion and abiding care. He invites readers into intimate explorations of place and spirit with clear, lyrical prose that we can follow like a map of outer and inner worlds.
—Todd Davis, author, *Coffin Honey*

Also by Tom Montgomery Fate:

Cabin Fever
Steady and Trembling
Beyond the White Noise
Challenging Boundaries in Central Appalachia
Rice and Beans and Hope

The Long Way Home

Detours and Discoveries

Tom Montgomery Fate

Ice Cube Press, LLC, Est. 1991
North Liberty, Iowa, USA

Thanks to the following journals and editors, where a version of these essays first appeared (sometimes under a different title):
    "Fishing for My Father": *Fourth Genre: Exploration in Nonfiction*, MSU Press (Laura Julier) and *The Chicago Tribune*.
    "The Presence of Absence": *The Chicago Tribune* (Jennifer Day).
    "Once More to the Lake, the Elephant and the Weasel": *The Chicago Tribune* (Rochell Sleets).
    "Weekend Monk," *River Teeth: A Journal of Narrative Nonfiction* (Joe Mackall). This essay was also selected as notable by Robert Atwan in *Best American Essays*.
    "Detours of Intention": *The Christian Century* (Elizabeth Palmer).
    "A Great Plenty": *The Christian Century* (Elizabeth Palmer) and *The Chicago Tribune* (excerpt).
    "The Rain on the Roof" is a revised and expanded version of an essay that first appeared in *Manoa*, Univ. of HI Press. And later appeared in *Across Cultures: A Reader for Writers*, (Ed. Sheena Gillespie, Allyn and Bacon) and *I'll Tell You Mine: Thirty Years of Essays from the Iowa Nonfiction Writing Program* (Eds. Hope Edelman and Robin Hemley, Univ. of Chicago Press).
    "Lost and Found in the Holy Land": *River Teeth: A Journal of Narrative Nonfiction* (Joe Mackall).
    "Travel That Takes You Home": *About Place* (Tammy Melody Gomez). The Black Earth Institute.

For my brothers,
Kendall, Paul, and Robin,
with gratitude

Quo Vadis

Sometimes I choose a cloud and let it
cross the sky floating me away.
Or a bird unravels its song and carries me
as it flies deeper and deeper into the woods.

Is there a way to be gone and still
belong? Travel that takes you home?

Is that life?—to stand by a river and go.

—William Stafford[1]

Contents

Detours Home:
An Introduction

Though we travel the world over to find the beautiful, we must carry it with us or we find it not.
—Ralph Waldo Emerson, Essays and Lectures

"Where do you call home?" a reporter once asked me in an interview for her newspaper.

"Iowa," I said.

"I thought you lived in Chicago," she replied.

"I do," I said. "But I'm *out of Iowa.* I'm from there, and I left there."

Then, I explained that I'd lived in Chicago for most of my life, but was slowly migrating back to Iowa the whole time. We lived in Hyde Park on Chicago's South Side for six years, then moved west to Oak Park, on the city-suburb border, for six years, and then to Glen Ellyn, a western burb, for another six years. We were returning to Iowa in 10-mile increments every six years, and would arrive at the Illinois-Iowa border when I was 104.

That westward migration stalled long ago. And since then, my idea of home has evolved. Now it's less a physical location than a kind of *belonging*. It's where my sense of being and my vast longings converge into one thing, something wordless—a kind of knowing, or belief, that I belong to Creation. I think of the Big Bluestem or Blazing Star on the prairie—how each plant is anchored by its searching—for water, for life. As patient and persistent as an Iowa farmer, the roots keep spiraling deeper into the darkness, on their way home.

I first came across this sense of home thirty years ago in a field studies course on the Pine Ridge Indian Reservation in South Dakota. In a sweat lodge, Francis White Lance, a medicine man, shared a core belief: *mitakuye oyasin*, meaning "all my relations," or *"I'm related to all that is."* Home as relationship—with birds and bugs and rivers and rocks, and other people. The phrase serves as a kind of closing prayer in Lakota ceremonies and connotes a home that is both physical and spiritual.

On the Pine Ridge, and elsewhere, I would learn that I had to leave Iowa to understand all that *home* could mean. This paradox suggests why that dull, flat, beautiful state now serves as my trailhead for a book of travel essays. Some of my journeys are "out of *Iowa*," as in *from* there, and rooted in my family and childhood, while others are "*out* of Iowa," as in *away from* there, and describe my treks through vastly different cultures. But these two strands of memory—"from" and "away from"—are sometimes woven into a single braid of meaning: travel that takes you home.

"We travel, initially, to lose ourselves," writes Pico Iyer, "and we travel, next, to find ourselves." Iyer has written a dozen travel books about remote exotic cultures—from the Philippines to Katmandu. I loved these books, but the one I reread is a critique of all the others: *The Art of Stillness: Adventures in Going Nowhere,* in which Iyer explores the necessity of the inner journey—of being lost, and found, and then lost again. This kind of searching is implied in the French origin of "travel"—*travail:* labor, toil; suffering, trouble. Travel involves struggle and a process of discovery and transformation.

§

"It matters not where or how far you travel," Henry David Thoreau writes, "the farther commonly the worse—but how much alive you are."[2] When I read *Walden* in college, this line confused me. So did his claiming that he'd "traveled a great deal in Concord," the small town where he lived his whole life. It made more sense many years later, when I reread the book and pondered my own life in a small town. Thoreau knew he *belonged* there. In hindsight, I was both sustained and limited by my life in small-town Iowa. But limitation as a gift, that can prompt a deeper attentiveness, and remind you what *enough* is.

In these essays, I first return to my Iowa stomping ground, where I felt at home, and then to far-flung cultures around the world, where I didn't. And along the way I keep searching for a spiritual home, for *mitakuye oyasin,* for a kind of belonging that I can carry with me wherever I go. But I am a slow and bumbling pilgrim. So whether bobbing in a canoe in the freezing rain with my son on a Canadian lake, or praying with Lakota elders in a sweat lodge in South Dakota, or trying to teach English in the Philippines—these are not stories of arrival. They are *detours*, my wayfinding through the wilderness of time and memory.

Fishing for My Father

We went fishing the first morning. I felt the same damp moss covering the worms in the bait can, and saw the dragonfly alight on the tip of my rod as it hovered a few inches from the surface of the water. It was the arrival of this fly that convinced me beyond any doubt that everything was as it always had been, that the years were a mirage and there had been no years.
—E.B. White, "ONCE MORE TO THE LAKE"

When I was 14, a single summer in Maquoketa, Iowa, felt like a lifetime. It was a county seat, a "big" small town with 5,000 people. Our little white ranch house was a quarter-mile from Highway 61, which leads to two cities: Dubuque, 30 miles north, and Davenport, 40 miles south. There you could shop in chain department stores like J.C. Penney or Montgomery Ward or even eat at McDonald's. Beyond the highway, thousands of acres of corn and soybeans unrolled into a green sprawl of endless farmland, which was marked and divided by a reliable grid of barbed wire and gravel roads. Along those roads and fence lines, the red-winged blackbirds perched, vigilant and ferocious, ready to attack any threat to their nests.

And high above them, the soaring red-tailed hawks described the wind, kiting on thermals while scanning the earth for a vole or cottontail. On those hot, dry days, I would watch a distant cloud of dust slowly crawl over the horizon, cross the hill by the sale barn, until it finally hit the blacktop and abruptly reappeared as some farmer's rusted pickup truck.

The highlight of the summer for me was always the county fair in July. My friends and I would eat hot dogs and cotton candy and ride the Rock-O-Plane and work the 25-cent cranes for prizes and huddle near the Tilt-A-Whirl, where we'd try to talk to some nervous clutch of gossipy Coke-sipping girls, who smelled of strawberry shampoo and apple lip gloss, and seemed unreachable, and were. The mystery of girls being so deep, we gave up pretty easily, and soon drifted over to the Grandstand, to watch the stock cars rev their smoking engines and wipe out in the mud. Or we wandered around amid the sweltering stench of a 4-H barn, trying to find a friend who was showing a prize steer.

The rest of the summer we mowed lawns and baled hay and roamed the town and surrounding farmlands on our bicycles with sweaty reckless abandon under the comfort of an enormous sky. Sometimes we brought our lunch, or fishing rods, or maybe a few cigarettes someone had stolen from their parents. The days were slow. And though we all had watches and clocks, the sun too measured our lives—the rising and fading light softening the edges of each day. Stores were not open 24/7, but 9-5, Monday through Saturday. For many, there was still a Sabbath, a day of rest.

My dad was the minister at the Congregational Church, so my older brother, Kendall, and I had to go every Sunday, after we finished our paper routes. I loved and hated being a preacher's kid. I liked the people and the potlucks, but that summer I was in 8th grade confirmation, and Dad was the teacher. He was smart but not much fun. In those days you didn't get treats or trophies or stickers for showing up. We had to read and discuss a lot of stuff—like the Psalms, the Beatitudes, and the Good Samaritan—and then write a brief paper. By the end of the class, I knew I was in trouble. Not because I didn't do the reading or write the papers, but because I didn't *believe*—or not the things I thought I should. On the Saturday morning before Confirmation Sunday, I walked into Dad's office all nervous and riding a river of hormones. My face was breaking out and my voice was breaking up, but I told him that I refused to be confirmed the next day with the other kids.

"Why!?" he asked. I told him I was unsure, that I might be one of those "egg-nostics," and just couldn't answer "yes" to all the required questions: Do you believe in God, the maker of heaven and earth? Do you accept Jesus Christ as your personal savior? Do you believe Jesus is the son of God?

Since it was a small town, everyone would know. None of the other five kids were backing out. No one ever did. It would be embarrassing for Dad, which is why he was pissed off: "Damn it. Why did you wait until the last minute?" I said

I didn't know for sure. He said he thought I was taking the questions too seriously. "How am I supposed to take them?" I asked. "Not so *literally*," he said.

We ranted and argued for a while, but then I finally reminded him about all the stuff he'd been teaching us. "What about 'the prison of certainty' and 'the hermeneutic of suspicion' and that 'Doubting Thomas' guy?'" I asked. At first, he was defensive, but before long he came around, and pretty soon we were both laughing at the irony of the whole thing. "Maybe the problem," Dad said finally, "is that you were the only one who was listening." And that was that. He finally accepted that my skepticism and doubt had come from his teaching. Even though I wasn't confirmed, Dad insisted I keep the shiny black, personally inscribed, King James Bible, which were provided for all the confirmands. So I did, but rarely opened it until many years later.

§

One of the joys of summer back then was fishing with Dad, usually just after supper. The river and woods on the edge of town were a different kind of church for him—a respite from his endless meetings and potlucks and hospital visits. But also from the dark cycles of depression that haunted him, that drugs could relieve but never resolve. Dad and Ken and I fished just below an old concrete dam on the Maquoketa River: on the bottom with bread balls for catfish and carp and with minnows for crappie and bass. The first time we went, I got bored and impatient. It was dusk and nothing was biting, except a cloud of mosquitoes. But my interest ignited when we began to catch fish—even one or two, and even small ones like bluegill and crappie. The magic of the dipping-then-disappearing bobber, and the sudden, hard tug of the line, soon hooked *me* on the rocky, burbling miracles of a river.

And I liked the rare, quiet time with my brother, and with Dad, who was happier and more relaxed when fishing. He was a good father, though often impatient and worried or preoccupied with his work—kind of like I am—meaning well, but too distracted to listen well. I remember him once coming down to the basement on Saturday afternoon, where I was blissfully watching *Let's Make a Deal* on TV, and eating Cheetos, and enjoying a lazy summer day. I could feel his stress—a familiar restlessness that had a mind of its own. He stomped around for a few minutes and then finally asked me if I'd mowed the lawn. I said no, that the grass was still wet, but I'd do it after the show. This frustrated him. "You can't spend the whole summer inside the house," he said, now angry. "You need to get out. *You're like a panther in a cage.*" The last line confused me, but I'd heard it before. It wasn't until years later I realized he was talking to himself, about how *he* felt—trapped and anxious.

But now I get it. Over the years I would sometimes argue with my son, Bennett. I remember once, when he was in junior high, that I claimed he was "addicted" to his cell phone. "That thing is glued to your hand," I said. "You never put it down." "I don't use it at school—and a lot less than my friends do," Bennett replied. "I don't care about your friends," I blustered.

"*You're distracted all the time.* You're always looking down at that thing and never fully present. Why can't you just relax?" It took me a few years to figure out, that whenever I said stuff like that I was *talking to myself*—just like my own dad—venting my confusion about the 24/7 digiphrenia of modern life, projecting my own anxieties at my son.

I still wonder if Dad took me fishing to teach me some patience or to restore his own, or if he even thought about such things. I sure didn't. But I do now—as a 60-something father who still struggles to find some light amid the darkness.

After planning to for several years, but never getting around to it, I finally took Bennett on a fishing trip when he started high school—a week of canoeing and camping in Canada with my older brother, Paul, and his son, Andy. I had made this trip before with my brothers, and my dad, but never with Bennett. Quetico Provincial Park is enormous—more than 2000 lakes, and a million acres of remote wilderness. So you kind of need to know where you're going and what you're doing.

Which is why I never have made the trip without one of my older brothers. And given that Bennett and I went canoeing as rarely as fishing, our minimal paddling skills concerned me a bit. So did being completely out of communication with other people for a week. No cell phones was a relief in one way, but what if someone broke their ankle?

The initial portage was a half-mile down a rocky trail through the woods. We carried in our food packs, tent, and other gear and loaded the canoes. They were packed tight, and as I crawled in I hooked myself on my own rod and lure—two treble hooks—one in my shirt, one in my thumb. I doubt this inspired much confidence in Bennett, but he was quiet and overlooked my swearing. Two hours later, when we entered an enormous lake and could barely negotiate the wind and whitecaps, he was still patient, and even quieter. I was quiet and anxious. So I did what I always do in such situations—followed my brother, and repeated his instructions to Bennett: "Paddle hard into the waves, then we'll turn quick and ride them in."

We changed our route, got out of the wind, found a nice site on a peninsula, and set up camp. For the next five days we paddled around and fished in a network of four lakes near our campsite. As we bobbed and drifted in the deep cold water, I kept giving Bennett advice: where to cast ("aim for that windy point at the drop-off; the walleye like to feed there"), what to use ("try that crawdad-colored crankbait"), how to work the lure ("get rid of the slack; reel, then let it drop"), and when he hooked a fish I'd say "be sure to set the hook" and "keep your rod tip up." Bennett patiently nodded at each of these gems.

§

One day, while fishing on shore, I made an odd maneuver: as I was casting, the top section of my rod went flying off into the lake—riding along the 8-pound test line like a mini graphite javelin—until it hit my well-tied tube jig fifty yards away. Then I proceeded to reel the top of my rod back in, along with the lure. Bennett didn't laugh or say a thing—until I started laughing. And then we both cut loose from the belly. That small, wondrous moment of hilarity, was a highlight of the week for me. It reminded me of my own dad, and how his raw honesty would compensate for his impatience, and the dark storms of depression when they blew in.

When I look back on the fishing trip now, I'm not sure why I couldn't recognize my emotional inheritance, or how I kept missing my son's resilient patience *with me* during that week. That was the quiet lesson of the trip.

Which is partly why, when I returned to the dam in Maquoketa last month, to scatter some of my dad's ashes in the river, I was not thinking just about him, but also about Bennett. I was wondering what Bennett might tell his kids someday, when he's my age, and reminiscing about that fishing trip he took with his old man to Canada 40 years ago. What would he remember? The four-pound smallmouth he landed? Or drinking the water right out of the lake? Or planning our days by the slow wheel of the sun? Or his dad's impatience and distraction and cycles of worry?

I tossed two fistfuls of ash—my father's body—into the wind. The two little grey clouds of dust drifted down into a powdery film onto the river. And as my dad dissolved into the shimmering water, it somehow felt like forgiveness—of us both. I stood there, imagining my dad, and son, and myself in the middle, all of us sitting on that thick slab of limestone along the bank. In my mind's eye, it was a hot and buggy day but we were resigned to it. So we all flicked our wrists and watched our skewered minnows fly out over the sparkling current, trailed by a red and white bobber and a double kerplunk. And there in the sun, we waited and watched, and dreamt of the world beneath the moving water.

The Presence
of Absence

Memory is the sense of loss, and loss pulls us after it.
—Marilynne Robinson, HOUSEKEEPING

I am still fishing for my father.

On the day he died he looked as run-down and parched as the tiny Nebraska farm he grew up on during the depression. Just as the dust storms of his youth had stolen the thin, rich topsoil from their farm, so had the quiet storm of Alzheimer's swept away his best thoughts and dreams from the landscape of memory. Nothing could grow or take root anymore in that barren place, in the drought of his mind.

A week earlier, my two older brothers, Paul and Rob, called and asked me to come to St. Paul, Minnesota, where they live, and where our dad was in a care center. It was time for hospice. Paul and Rob had managed the day-to-day slog of Dad's mental decline for two years—the maze of doctors and caretakers and meds and how to pay for it all. A few months prior, when Dad escaped his room, and locked himself outside in his underwear in a snowy parking lot on a freezing January night, they moved him to a memory unit.

That was a sad place. All the windows were locked and alarmed and the entrance door required a digital code. Without the rudder of memory, my father and the nine residents in his unit all seemed adrift in a tiny boat on a wild, infinite sea—yet unconcerned about finding their way back to shore. Whenever I visited and had dinner with them, I wondered how I appeared to them: a dim light off in the distance toward which they might row for a few seconds? And I wondered what I would do, if it were me, and if I could still decide. That is, if I couldn't recognize my family or friends, or remember what and who I loved, would I want to keep going?

We didn't know how long Dad would live—a few days perhaps. On the day he died, we all took turns sitting with him. That afternoon his eyes were closed, his breathing unsteady, and he could barely swallow. Sometimes he'd startle awake for a minute out of his sleep and look at me with concern. I tried to comfort him but didn't know how. What could he see?

So I just sat there in that little room with the gaunt shell of his body, and his last whispers of thought, and tried to pray. But I'm not good at prayer, so my mind began to wander. I thought of the memoir I'd just finished reading: *The Presence of Absence*. At age 81, Doris Grumbach writes of an epiphany she had at 27, and describes her life-long search to relive it—to rediscover the presence of God. After long presuming that all "religious experience" was like her epiphany—she stumbles upon psychotherapist James Hillman's idea that "absence is the first form of knowing." Finally, she accepts the possibility of a God even without the proof she has been seeking.

Her search for proof didn't interest me as much as the paradoxical title. While "the presence of absence" may describe God, it better describes Alzheimer's, a disease that leaves a person physically present, but mentally absent. And we had all been watching it take hold of Dad for several years. The growing absence: the widening gaps between thoughts, the nonsensical unfinished sentences, the angry outbursts at nurses. Then, finally, he could no longer dress or feed himself, and his mind began to seem as dark and cavernous as an empty church.

It was then, just beyond Dad's bed, and outside his third floor window, maybe 20 feet away, that the miracle occurred: a snow-white squirrel appeared at the tip of a long, twisted bur oak limb. It peered in at us for a second, but then raced down the black trunk in a crazed scramble, dashed across the yard and disappeared. Though I'm skeptical when others mention such stories, I wondered if the squirrel was some sort of sign—or some kind of angel or ghost—the kind of "proof" that Grumbach had so longed for. But what then would the rodent-angel be proving?

I remember once discussing miracles with a religion professor in college. We were reading an essay by the philosopher, Baruch Spinoza, and considering whether miracles were evidence of God. Trying to summarize the work for me, Professor Holstein put it this way: "Why would God break His own natural law (snow white squirrels?) to prove to another of His creatures (humans) that He existed?" I liked this argument. But still, it was odd. After all, there *were* no white squirrels. I'd never heard of or seen one before. And given the timing, it did feel like a sign. But of what? I started to question what I had actually seen. I thought again of a Lakota mentor, Francis White Lance, who liked to say "Believing is seeing," reversing the old adage, and implying that *seeking* the Great Spirit enabled *seeing* the Great Spirit. Some believe the same is true with dead loved ones.

I used to teach "Buckeye," in my writing classes, a popular essay by Scott Russell Sanders, in which he claims that a soaring hawk he saw one sunny afternoon was also his dead father. "It was a red-tailed hawk for sure; and it was also my father," Sanders writes. "Not a symbol of my father, not a reminder, not a ghost, but the man himself, right there, circling in the air above me."[3] After reading the essay at a conference I attended, Sanders mentioned that dozens of people had written him about having a similar experience—about encountering a dead spouse or parent or sibling in a crow or fox or some other animal.

But my father was not dead. And soon my faith in the would-be miracle waned and logic intruded. Unlike Sanders, I didn't sense a spiritual presence in an animal. And I would later learn, that though uncommon, there were many white squirrels in St. Paul, as it was a genetic mutation of the grey squirrel. Unlike Francis White Lance, I was a seeker, but not a seer. Still, the apparition of the squirrel ghost had left me intensely focused on the natural world outside my father's bedside window, a world which it seemed he was both leaving and returning to.

The rest of the afternoon a cold rain blew through the trees, and I kept looking out Dad's window and wishing that he could too. It was Cinco de Mayo. Everything was green and budding, eager to be born. Spring: the season of remembering, when all the parts—the humus and detritus and water and sunlight and carbon dioxide—all *come together again* to make new life from decay and death. It was Dad who first told me that the word religion means "to tie, or bind together again" (*re-ligare*). And this went beyond holy books and holy wars and holy buildings; a religion included *all* living things. So maybe the white squirrel *was* a miracle, because it was *bound* to the cycle of creation, of remembering. And so was Dad. Though it was not belonging I felt that day; it was the fear of separation.

Since Dad had been a pastor for almost 50 years, he'd spent a lot of time in care centers like this one—doing what I was doing—sitting with his parishioners in their last days and hours. But the longer I sat there, the more lost I felt, and the more I wondered what he would have done if he were me. Finally, I put one hand on the warm dome of his skull and the other on his dry, stubbled face, and cried. Mainly from grief I think, but also from gratitude—for a life well-lived, and a man well-loved.

Then I placed my hand on Dad's chest and felt the rise and fall of a lung, and put the other hand on his heart, and felt the faint burble of an 88-year-old pump, and the limits of blood and flesh and bone, of *body*, and the limits of *mind*, of the electrochemical charges that create thought, emotion, memory, which got me wondering about *spirit*, and how these three parts of a person converge, or don't—in life, and in death.

Somehow the idea of "spirit" turned me back to Grumbach, and the presence of absence. I was wondering how Dad might respond to her questions. Ever since my non-confirmation all those years ago, I had heard him say it: "Doubt is not the opposite of faith, but a part of it. The point of faith is not answers, but meaning. Live in the questions, in the mystery."

Then Dad stirred again. His eyes opened, and they seemed less distant. He slightly turned his head toward me, barely squeezed my hand, and in an airy, labored whisper said "luf" or "luh" or "huv." Or was it "love"? He said it twice—with much effort—and I sensed a faint spark of recognition, a *presence*. But who can know for sure? Then his eyes closed again, and he fell back asleep.

An hour later, my brother Kendall arrived, from Iowa, to relieve me. He soon noticed a little blue sponge that the nurse had left, moistened it, and began to swab Dad's dried lips and mouth. I hadn't noticed the sponge, but was glad Ken did, as the moisture seemed to comfort Dad. His eyebrows lifted slightly, and his breathing seemed a bit more regular. But it was time for me to go. So I grabbed my coat and keys, kissed my dad goodbye, and walked through the rain out to my car. On the long drive home I listened to James Taylor, Stevie Nicks, Springsteen, Joan Baez—to old, comforting favorites— and tried to imagine the world without my father, but could not. Late that night, soon after I'd arrived back in Chicago, Ken called to say that Dad had died. The drought had ended. Our father had blown away.

§

Weeks later, while preparing a talk for the funeral, I wondered about my father's last word to me. I'm not certain that it was "love." But I want to *believe* it was. And belief is a different kind of knowing. It's subjective, like most of our remembering. Our perception of our past lives is an ongoing act of interpretation which involves the whole of our intellect, including the imagination.

I've had to learn this as a writer, but it was never more clear to me than while watching my father's memory dry up and blow away. The things he lost that mattered most were not dates or facts, not the provable or the certain. Not the days of the week, or his social security number, or the number of congregants in the last church he served.

What mattered was the wild swirl of stories that he carried—that holy reservoir of images and moments, of love and loss—that told him, and others, who he was. Shucking corn on hot summer days until his hands bled during the Dust Bowl, and swimming in the Little Blue River for relief. Rushing home from the Navy, at 19, to be with his dying father in his last days. And there finding his oldest brother, George, sobbing in the hay barn—the only time he'd ever seen him cry. Arriving at the University of Chicago Divinity School just after World War II to begin studies, and feeling like he'd landed on a different planet. Preaching a sermon in Ames, Iowa, in 1964, against Barry Goldwater and the war in Vietnam that would prompt such a backlash, he would have to leave that church.

Just four stories, four moments among thousands. Yet all flow from one life—with its myriad turns and twists and winding streams of meaning—and will keep unfolding in anyone who knows my father. The stories won't die unless we stop telling them.

§

The funeral was on a sunny, hot June morning at the First Congregational Church of Iowa City, Iowa, where my parents had attended for fifteen years. A dozen or so friends from Maquoketa made the 75-mile drive to say goodbye to their old pastor, to remember their shared lives. After the funeral there was coffee and sandwiches and many long conversations. But then our family and friends all got back in their cars and returned to their homes. And that was when the waves of grief hit hardest. I'm not sure why. That line from Grumbach's book returned to me: "absence is the first form of knowing."

Awash in sadness, I soon began to sort through some of Dad's old journals and his favorite books, hoping to restore a sense of his presence. I finally settled on two books. The first was *The Courage to Be,* by Paul Tillich, a renowned philosopher who lectured at The University of Chicago Divinity School when Dad was a student there. He bought the book when it first came out in 1952. I read the same copy (with his annotations) nearly 40 years later, when I was assigned the book as a student at Chicago Theological Seminary—just across the street from the Divinity School. Having just graduated from the writing program at the University of Iowa, and completed a book about my experiences in war-torn Nicaragua, I found Tillich deathly boring. I wanted to retitle his book: *The Courage to Be Completely Unreadable,* or maybe *The Courage to Be a Self-Absorbed Intellectual Who is Out of Touch with Everything that Matters.*

Given Tillich's distant, theoretical language, I was surprised to see Dad had underlined about half of the book. I presumed he either thought all of those ideas were important, or couldn't determine which ones were. Here is one of those underlined sentences: "Ontic and spiritual self-affirmation must be distinguished but they cannot be separated." The whole book is like that—an ocean of abstraction. On page 42, I long ago added what I think is my only notation in the book—a smiley face—to have some fun with Dad and our daunting surname. "*Fate* is the rule of contingency," Tillich writes. "And the anxiety about fate is based on the finite being's awareness of being contingent in every respect, of having no ultimate necessity." While in seminary, I sent a letter to my dad including this sentence, along with this note: "I'm not sure you knew this, Dad, but I just discovered that Tillich references you in *The Courage to Be*. He seems to think the reason your congregation is anxious about you is because you have no "ultimate necessity." Dad got a kick out of that.

The other book I picked up that morning was Marilynne Robinson's novel, *Gilead*. The book meant a lot to my dad, in part, because the protagonist is also a small-town Iowa pastor. And the meaning is deepened because Robinson and Dad were long-time friends and attended the same church. For a brief period, during an interim, he was her pastor.

In a remembrance, that Robinson wrote for the Iowa City newspaper, she said some nice things about my father, but she also did something that *Gilead* did—celebrated the small-town pastor.

"The role of pastor is ancient and complex, especially difficult now," she wrote, "when institutional religion seems to hold a more tenuous place in society than it has through most of history. Rev. Russ Fate exemplified the qualities that have made the role honored and valued." And later: "There is no way of reckoning the value good pastors bring to the lives and communities that are privileged to know them, or the extent of their influence, which is usually quiet, unfolding over time."

The next week I began to reread *Gilead*, which helped to dull the grief, and to loosen some hard knots of memory. The novel is a series of letters written by Rev. John Ames to his young son in Gilead, Iowa (a fictional town). And though the work is set in 1957, it somehow captures the spiritual ethos of my own childhood a decade later, when I also grew up in a small Iowa town, also the son of a Congregational minister. The two towns are quite different, but the Gilead church reminded me of my dad's: a deeply flawed and profoundly beautiful community of farmers and mechanics and school teachers and salesmen who worked hard and took care of each other.

Given my intimate knowledge of the life of a small-town pastor, I was thankful for how carefully Robinson explored that life. Rev. Ames, the protagonist, is a good listener, and a quiet, dutiful intellectual—a pastor in the best sense. He differs greatly from his grandfather (also a minister), who was less pastor than prophet—a passionate, uncompromising truth-seeker, who was always stirring the pot.

I sometimes noticed this conflict in my dad. What was his role—pastor or prophet? Was he a patient seer or an impatient seeker? Sometimes he would walk *in front* of his flock, making pronouncements and passionately condemning injustice or espousing some new theological insight as a mandate for action. But he also knew that his University of Chicago education wouldn't easily translate in Maquoketa—that theologians like Tillich and Reinhold Niebuhr might be less important than corn prices and high school football. "You don't need all those books to be a good minister," one parishioner wrote him. "Preach from the heart, not the head." The unsigned note was slipped under the door of his study. Dad mentioned this to me many years after it happened. "The heart and the head are dependent on each other," he said, still bothered by the note. People also commented on how Dad overused the phrase "and, in conclusion," noting that his various "conclusions" sometimes constituted half of the sermon. And given his tin ear, whenever he forgot to turn off the mike during hymns, and loudly carried the melody in the wrong direction, he would always hear about it. All such comments hurt Dad deeply. He couldn't let them go or roll with the punches. Like most small-town ministers, he was expected to be a self-assured, virtuous role model, but wasn't always. He was just as human and flawed and vulnerable as everyone else.

Which is probably why he knew, like any good shepherd, to spend most of his time walking *behind* the flock, wading through all their shit and assisting anyone who got trampled or left behind. The essential skill was not speaking but listening—an aptitude that I presume is related to prayer, to listening for God amid the routine and exhaustion of everyday life. A small-town pastor has no choice but to pursue a theology of daily life—of endless potlucks and coffee shop discussions and late-night prayers in some darkened hospital room.

Several years ago, at her home in Iowa City, I asked Marilynne Robinson about such a life. Wondering about my dad, I asked if her protagonist, Rev. John Ames, wasn't kind of "stuck" in Gilead, if his theological training and intellectual gifts weren't misaligned or somewhat wasted in such a small, backwater town.

"There isn't any necessary relation between the scope of one's mind and where they live," she said. "Ames is highly educated. He knows what books to read, he knows what's going on in the world, and thus is intellectually sophisticated. A life lived well is never wasted no matter what the scale of that life is. He lives toward God. And there is no way of measuring that." Somehow our whole conversation boiled down to those last three sentences, to the scale of the immeasurable, to the process of living toward God—whatever that might mean.

As I continued to read Dad's copy of *Gilead* that day, I couldn't help but notice that unlike *The Courage to Be*, there were only a half dozen passages underlined, and there were few marginal notes. The last lines Dad marked in *Gilead* still haunt and comfort me.

"Wherever you turn your eyes the world can shine like transfiguration. You don't have to bring a thing to it except a willingness to see. Only, who could have the courage to see it?"

Not the courage to be, but the courage to see. Next to the passage, he scratched the word "faith" in the margin.

These lines come at the end of the book and of John Ames' life. They returned to me at the end of my father's. I don't have the kind of faith he did, or that Ames did. Sometimes "the presence of absence" is an apt description of my religious belief. Dad felt a calling as a pastor and a prophet, while I'm more drawn to the artist and activist. Yet we shared a core belief in *a willingness to see*, and in writing, as a way of seeing, as an act of faith in creation. Which is why I remember my father with words, with story. Words keep him present. And my last word is always the same as the one he said to me. Love.

Weekend Monk

*The silence is all there is. It is the alpha and the omega,
it is God's brooding over the face of the waters; it is the
blinded note of the ten thousand things, the whine of
wings. You take a step in the right direction to pray to
this silence, and even to address the prayer to "World."
Distinctions blur. Quit your tents. Pray without ceasing.*
—Annie Dillard, Teaching a Stone to Talk

A year after my father's death, I visited a Benedictine Abbey
near Maquoketa. Dad had gone there when I was in high
school, found it meaningful, and told me I should try it sometime. Forty years later I finally did—in homage to Dad, but
also to calm the parts of him that still twisted in me. Dad was
a kind and loving person, but not patient or meditative. He
was more on the anxious, harried side—like me. At the time, I
was pretty sure I would be a terrible monk, which may be why
the idea of the monk was so alluring: the uber-committed, ul-
tra-humble, self-sacrificial psalm chanter who never leaves his
community or home ground. *Stability*, in place and mind. So
I wondered if I could be a *weekend monk*—somehow packing
the lifelong commitment to prayer and work and community
into an occasional three-day weekend. I gave it a try.

§

I couldn't watch both the road and the pulsing blue GPS dot on my iPhone map, and got lost somewhere near Dubuque. I'd accidentally spun the whole map upside down with my index finger, so nothing made sense. North was no longer north. I grew up just 30 miles away, but the dusty county road winding through the endless cornfields looked like a hundred others I'd traveled. And my internal compass had gotten less reliable as I'd grown reliant on digital ones. But finally, with a paper map, I found Monastery Road and followed it to an asphalt lane which led through a row of towering white pines, and opened to the yellow stone entrance of the New Melleray Abbey. Like many Iowa communities, it was small, in the middle of nowhere, and quite beautiful.

A pamphlet for guests in a rack near the Abbey's entrance serves as a guide for visitors:

> *The monks describe themselves as "Christians professing the Rule of St. Benedict." As you make your retreat at New Melleray, you will learn more about the monks, the Rule of Saint Benedict, and a life oriented to contemplative prayer.*

That's partly why I had gone—to take another crack at prayer. It never really worked for me, but I used to practice more—in seminary, which is where I first read about the Rule of St. Benedict in Thomas Merton's books. In the 6th century, Benedict of Nursia, an ascetic monk, who lived in a cave in Italy for three years, wrote a book of rules for monastic communities. It prescribes a life of prayer that is separate from "the world," obedient to Christian ideals, and under the authority of an abbot. The Rule later became the guidebook for monastic life, and for fifteen hundred years, monasteries around the globe have followed it, including New Melleray.

When I arrived at the Guestmaster's office to get my room assignment, Fr. Jonah, a stocky, balding, 70-something monk, was leaning on his walker and thumbing through a folder. He clearly didn't expect me, but quickly found my reservation. "You're in 218 for three nights," he said. "There are no keys. Meals are downstairs in the refectory after prayers." When he asked where I was from, I mentioned that I'd taken classes at Catholic Theological Union (CTU)—a respected seminary. "We call that the Cesspool of Theological Uncertainty," he said smiling.

Given this barb, and my own eclectic theology, I didn't respond. For me, the "study of God" (*ology theo*), and religion itself, *is* rooted in uncertainty, in questions. And I'm not the only one. A recent PEW study found that while 56% of US adults believe in a God as described by the Bible, 90% believe in "some kind of higher power," a term that has limitless possibilities. [4] And words like "belief" and "faith" connote different things to different people. For many, the opposite of faith is doubt. For me, it's *certainty*.

After my five-minute orientation with Fr. Jonah was over, I had a "What am I doing here?" moment. Was I some ridiculous wannabe monastic? A weekend monk!? One of those distracted frenetic people seeking a conveniently brief yet deeply inspiring retreat from normal life?

What if the Abbey had a special program for people like me? That's just what I needed—one more terminal grad degree in the humanities. I can imagine the promo on their website:

Accelerated Low Residency Online M.A.M.
(Masters in Monastics)
Benedictine Monk Certification.
Only three weekend retreats required. No vows of stability!
We bend "The Rule" so you can go to school!

I thanked the Guestmaster, went to my car, grabbed my bag and books, and climbed the stairs to my "cell." Cell. I like this word. It turns a monastery into a prison, a pilgrim into a prisoner. It highlights the isolation of the monks and artists and other willing captives who seek to be creatively *freed* in their confinement, in their boiled-down lives. They are not "doing time," but making it. That's what the word poet *(poetes)* means: "maker." An artist too has faith—in their search for meaning amid the mystery of creation—in how they trust and listen to the stillness.

And it *was* still—eerily quiet. The monks took no vows of silence, yet no one spoke to me. The other two weekend monks I had seen only smiled, and meekly—probably not wanting to appear like what we were: spiritual tourists. The monks I passed nodded reassuringly and *knowingly.* What did they know? Couldn't someone speak up?

Room #218 was a spotless 7 by 10-foot room with a single bed and small pine desk. I sat down at the desk and let out a deep sigh. *Now what do I do?* How would I calm my racing mind? In spite of my good intentions, at that moment I could neither write nor pray. I was lost. So I kept waiting, and trying to listen, and not to think about the Iowa-Iowa State game. The kick-off for the nationally televised game was in an hour. Was driving to a pub in Dubuque to watch the game completely out of the question?

§

A writer's faith is a commitment to a process of discovery, which is laced with doubt and mystery. And there is always a kind of sacred confusion, whether waiting for words at your desk, or in some forest, or in some empty pew. But after nineteen minutes had clicked by on my digital watch, my anxiety swelled into the same old question: What am I doing here? I tried to meditate by focusing on my breath, but I had grown dependent on the "Calm" app on my cell phone (which I left in the car during my stay). So I was antsy. And God, it was quiet. Or maybe I should say, *God was quiet.* "The silence of God is God," Carolyn Forche writes.[5] And I get it. A prayer is not a phone call.

I returned to the pamphlet's instructions for guests:

The word "monk" actually comes from the Greek word Monos meaning "one alone." The monks and nuns are separated from ordinary society: the bustle of business, the chaos of the streets, and the blare of the media.

I sometimes like the chaos and bustle, but not the "blare of the media." Not Facebook envy. Not being *the only one* who was not dining in Venice at sunset or swimming with dolphins in Florida or on a winter cruise in the Mediterranean. The constant lure of social media is the opposite of prayer—it tips me off-center. Yet, when I lost access, I kind of missed it.

In place of the mad rush and noise of modern life, the monastery is a place where the monks and nuns can be "one alone" even though they live, work and pray together as a community.

Work and prayer: that was Benedict's motto (*ora et labora*) and it's the bedrock of a Benedictine community. The "work" is both a sacred discipline and necessary for the monastery's economic survival. Some communities have raised sheep, or made bread, or jam, or furniture, or honey, or all of the above. New Melleray sustains itself through making caskets, which are crafted from pine and oak and cherry, and much in demand.

But prayer is at the heart of monastic life and requires intensive focus—mono-tasking. Each day the Monks pray the Liturgy of the Hours, a cycle of seven prayers at prescribed times:

> *3:30 AM Vigils*
> *6:30 AM Lauds*
> *9:15 AM Terce*
> *11:45 AM Sext*
> *1:45 PM None*
> *5:30 PM Vespers*
> *7:30 PM Compline*

Some bewildered weekend monks, like me, try to follow this cycle with the real, full-time monks. That was my plan, with the help of an alarm clock, which they told me to bring (rather than a cell phone). Do you remember alarm clocks? Unlike cell phones, they don't have hundreds of soothing, whispering ring tones to choose from. The loud, angry buzzing sound at 3:20 AM actually *alarmed* me that first night. I bolted out of bed, thinking "Fire!" and that I had to get out of the building.

Blurry-eyed, I pulled on my pants and a flannel shirt and rinsed my face in the sink. At 3:25 AM the tower bell bong-bong-bonged, and I stumbled down the stairs to the chapel and the visitors' pews. Just one other well-meaning non-monk appeared—a middle-aged man in jeans and a forest green sweater, who looked wide awake. We gave each other the requisite meek smiles of recognition. The organist began to play, and the monks, some with canes and walkers, filed in the chancel ahead of us—two parallel rows of 12 old men. Soon they began to chant the assigned Psalms for Vigils, their haunting, barely melodic voices echoing off the stone floor and high ceiling. I didn't have the daily order of service—or the words to the Psalms. Nor did the other person. And I was not given any instructions. I soon realized that we outsiders, in the visitors' pews—who numbered between one and five during my stay—were both a part of and apart from the community. We took communion and joined in the common prayers, but mostly we prayed by listening to the monks pray. This felt strange and humbling and sometimes beautiful. Though it highlighted the tourism—our distant *looking at,* rather than the riskier *seeing with.* Which is what is so appealing about *tours*—the easy, unearned access to meaning, the fun stuff without the hard stuff, and there is less boredom and waiting. But I knew that waiting is at the heart of writing, and prayer. So while a tour is a pleasant, predictable distraction from normal life, the daily journey of the artist/monk is often a detour, with the destination unclear.

At the end of day one, I calculated that with all seven sessions I had spent a total of three and a half hours in prayer. My need to tally up my prayer time is embarrassing, but three and a half hours may be close to my *annual* prayer allotment, given that the rote 10-second pre-meal gratitude prayer has become my staple. So this was an adjustment and an education. But I got it: the regularity of the prayers ensures you'll never think about much else—except the next prayer session, and God—which is the whole point.

At first it felt odd that prayer—an immeasurable attempt to listen for the mystery of God— should be so regimented, so carefully timed. But for the monks, the art of prayer is like the art of writing: you can't do it only when inspired. Rather, it is the core practice that orders daily life: the discipline of waiting, and believing in a creative process of discovery.

Yet how ironic that this fervent quest for order, and to regularize prayer, is what led the Benedictines to invent the first mechanical clock. Just as New Melleray does now, the Benedictine Abbeys in 12th century Europe used bells (*clocca*) to call the monks to prayer. The problem, though, was accuracy—how to ring the community into prayer at the same prescribed times each day. "Natural time"—time measured by the cycles of the sun and changing seasons—was irregular. The precision and reliability of the mechanical clock also enabled the monks to replace the cyclical seasonal calendar, which focused on the past, with the idea of the "schedule," which focused on planning the future.

Not surprisingly, by the middle of the 14th century the lure of the Benedictine clock, of measured time, spread outside the monastery walls to the world of commerce. This introduced "the idea of regular production, regular working hours and a standardized project," writes Neil Postman. "The clock was invented by men who wanted to devote themselves more rigorously to God; it ended as the technology of greatest use to men who wished to devote themselves to the accumulation of money."[6] By the 15th century, giant clocks had replaced the church bell towers as the social hub of the town square, and "Holy Days" evolved into "Holidays."

But that was all long ago. Today most of the remaining Benedictine communities, like New Melleray, are dying out, as there are few new recruits. At their peak, in the early fifties, New Melleray had 150 monks, but now there are 30. They survive through religious tourism (for people like me), through renting out their spaces for conferences, and through their casket business. And today, rather than being on the cutting edge of time technology, New Melleray is still centered on the *clocca*, a clanging bell calling the monks back to prayer, back to God.

Aside from the regimented prayers, I spent my days at New Melleray reading, writing, and walking. For me, walking is the purest form of prayer, as the physical rhythm of my body calms and opens my mind to deeper listening. In motion, the body, mind and spirit seem to more readily merge, to become one being. And while I have not learned how to "pray without ceasing," as Annie Dillard advocates, I admire the intention. And a long walk through a forest, or pasture, or some dried-out creek bed, is as close as I get to this idea—to praying/listening *without measure*, without any sense of time or destination.

On my last day at the Abbey, I discovered a book in the Abbey library by a poet I've long admired: Jane Hirshfield. Her words lingered as I prepared to leave.

"The desire of monks and mystics is not unlike that of artists: to perceive the extraordinary within the ordinary by changing not the world but the eyes that look…." [7]

To say an artist sees the extraordinary in the "ordinary" is a cliché. But connecting that word to monks evokes its religious origin. "Ordinary" comes from "order"—as in a monastic order. An ordinand has just been ordained to a ministerial order. "Ordinary Time" refers to the Catholic liturgical year, except for the "highlights": Advent, Christmas, Lent, and Easter. The "Ordinary" of the Catholic Mass refers to those parts of the Mass that don't change. The structure and discipline in a monk's daily life is aligned with the ordinary (sacred) structure and discipline of his faith. Monks refer to the routine of their daily prayer cycle as "sanctified time."

The next morning I cleaned my room and packed my bag. The three long days had been both inspiring and frustrating. I don't know if I got any better at praying or writing or seeing. My faith was still lacking, still defined by doubt, and confusion, and hope. But I kept trying, and maybe that's the point. The artful *practice* of faith and writing is all there is. Revision is all there is. No arrival.

When I got to my car, I quickly dug my cell phone out of the glove compartment, and felt a familiar pang of excitement. But the battery was dead. And there was no charging cord. No GPS. So I pulled out a paper map of Iowa and considered the two routes south to Maquoketa: Highway 61, a straight four-lane with a 70 mph limit, and county Y-21, a meandering two-lane with a 50 mph limit. I took the road less traveled, rolled down my windows and slowly cruised through the sunlit fields and woodlands. The air was cool and dry, the empty sky endless. Some farmer was burning brush, and the smoke mingled with the sour stink of manure and the sweet scent of freshly cut hay. Along the fence line cattle grazed on the frosted weeds.

Detours of Intention

*I regard poets and monks as the best degenerates
in America. Both have a finely developed sense of the
sacred potential in all things.*
—Kathleen Norris, THE CLOISTER WALK

A few years later I had a sabbatical at another Benedictine Abbey: St. John's University in Collegeville, Minnesota. I knew about the Abbey from a Kathleen Norris book, which she wrote there thirty years ago. *Dakota*—a "spiritual geography"—turned these boring old plains into sacred ground. The book felt like a midwestern *Walden* to me. This mattered, as I've lived in Iowa and Illinois my whole life. *Dakota* also resonated with me at the time, because I'd just completed two graduate degrees back-to-back—in creative writing and religion—and was still not sure how/if they might align. Poet-monks like Norris and Thoreau gave me hope.

The worst part of the sabbatical at St. John's was that it began in mid-January in central Minnesota. The best part was that it was only an hour and a half from my 92-year-old mom's care center in St. Paul. I could drive over and see her every weekend. I usually went on Sundays, so we could go to church and out to lunch. On one visit, after we'd eaten, Mom asked what I was doing with my time at St. John's, and so I read the first four paragraphs of the piece I was working on. That was how long it took her to fall asleep. When she nodded back awake I asked her what she thought. She had no idea about what I'd read, but after she got her bearings, like always, she tried to reassure me: "I'm just *so* glad you're here, Tom. It's good you're *here*."

§

Four o'clock PM. Twelve below zero. I had just arrived at the Abbey, but it was an hour before evening prayers, so I took a hike around Lake Sagatagan. My destination was Stella Maris ("Star of the Sea"), a tiny red brick chapel built by the monks more than a century ago. It was much farther than I remembered. Or maybe it was just cold. Or the wind, or the snow. I last visited the Abbey in the summer. Then people were swimming and kayaking.

As I walked, I noticed a single trail of footprints led out to the middle of the lake, where a man kneeled on the ice in the brutal wind. He was very still. Waiting. Ice-fishing I assumed. Or maybe praying. Maybe both. That day they seemed like the same thing. Any fish that appeared would surely be a sign from God. When I got closer to the bank, I could make out the auger he'd used to drill the hole, and a little rod and a silver can. But no fish, or shelter from the wind.

A half-hour later I arrived at the chapel. It was warmer inside—maybe 15 above. I said a prayer of gratitude. That's why I had come, on the cusp of a sabbatical—to offer thanks. "Thank you for *Shmita*, for Sabbath time to write and walk and pray," I said to the empty room, to the frozen stones and small wooden pew.

It was then I noticed the orange and blue rays of sunlight flooding through a stained glass window. The warm shafts of color felt like answers to a question I didn't know how to ask. So I stopped trying, and instead took a picture of the window and the wild spokes of light with my cell phone—a photo that later befuddled me. The image just didn't make sense. The rainbow of warm colors was gone, and was replaced by a ball of eerie green light. Where did that come from? Why didn't the i-camera *see* what my eye-camera saw? Had I missed some sacred revelation that afternoon in the chapel? And if so, of what? Was it an apparition of the Holy Spirit? Or had God just appeared to me as a green apple sun? What could it mean?

Over the years many "seekers" have taken photos of holy apparitions in unexpected places: Jesus appears on a pancake, a burnt tortilla, or a chicken nugget. The Virgin Mary appears on a slice of pizza. A swirling blue-green God magically haunts a photo of the northern lights. Should I have called the news media to share my own miraculous encounter with the divine?

No, it turns out. A photographer friend later explained: not holy apparition, but wholly accident—a common mechanical misfire known as "lens flare." The sun causes a reflection on the lens, which is misread by the camera's sensors, confusing its digital brain. This got me thinking: Is a technological accident—the mismeasurement of light, and the beauty it reveals—any less of a natural miracle than a rainbow? The digital brain is not human, but the human brain designed it. The lens of the eye looks through the lens of the camera in order to see better? Or to see more? A green apple god? A white squirrel? If believing is seeing, as Francis White Lance claimed, then I believe in the beauty of Creation—that in seeking it I might enable seeing it. Seek and you shall *see*. Maybe.

Once, while walking through the woods in Michigan, in the middle of the night, a full moon filtered through the forest canopy of white pine and red oak, and cast shimmering patches of light on the forest floor below. The moon is 238,900 miles away from the earth. Talk about miracles. I tried to frame that moment with my iPhone camera, but it would not record it. I took several shots of those soft flickering blotches of light on the ground, and tried different settings, but nothing worked. I focused and refocused and framed and reframed each image. But they all came back as black squares of nothing. Darkness. The beauty of the light could not be captured by my iPhone8 camera, only by the blood, muscle and nerve of a much older model.

§

"Attentiveness without an aim is the supreme form of prayer," writes the French mystic Simone Weil. This sort of makes sense to me. The poet and the monk both attempt to live in a perpetual prayer of attention. But no one has the focus or patience to be *fully* attentive and present. *No one's perfect.* If I were a verb tense, I would be *imperfect,* and *present*: an "unfinished" action happening now. As in "I am trying to fish" or "I am trying to pray"—both of which require waiting and wondering.

As I sat there in the chapel, hunched on the frozen pew, I considered why it was so hard to believe that *everyone* is unfinished—and beautiful. I used to tell my writing students that beauty is recognized and defined by *flaw,* not flawlessness. It's about difference and uniqueness, not the cookie cutter shape or symmetry of TV models for underwear or face cream. It's the sharp crook in the nose, the oddly tilted smile, or how one eyebrow arches up in disbelief all by itself.

But recognizing the beauty in our daily lives requires a deep attentiveness. And that is harder now, since we tend to reward distraction—multi-present multi-tasking. As we twitter and snap and text, our FOMO and insecurity grow, though our attention spans shrink. Waiting, and paying attention, have become countercultural.

Which is partly what made the pandemic so difficult: we had to wait for months for a hug, or a Covid test, or a vaccine, or rent money, or a new job. So while my time at St. John's did not prepare me for the pandemic, it didn't hurt. I went there to *practice*—to wait and wonder—like Norris and Thoreau, and that guy out there on the ice. Because that's what monks and poets do. They practice. They are unfinished. They don't arrive.

Another poet-monk, Thomas Merton, visited the Abbey in 1956, and walked to the chapel: "Yesterday I spent most of the afternoon in the quiet woods behind Stella Maris Chapel," he wrote, "reading, thinking and realizing the inadequacy of both reading and thinking."[8] Merton, a Trappist, may be the most well-known monk of the modern era. In part because he wrote 50 books and read voraciously his whole life. Often he writes of the paradox of a monk's life: they belong to the world by retreating from it. And, like the Benedictines, the Trappists also take a vow of *stability*—to stay put in one abbey for their whole lives.

Walking back around the lake that day, I felt the "inadequacy" Merton mentioned, as I pondered what I was hoping to write—stories of *travel*, both physical and spiritual. Not stories of arrival—but of being lost, and found, and lost again. Not only "a journey into space," as Nelle Morton once wrote, "but a journey into presence." Not tours, but unmarked detours. *Detours of intention,* which can be read two ways: sometimes I chose the route, but more often it chose me.

A prayer is also a detour of intention. We don't know where we're going. We choose to wait, and to listen, but for how long? Five minutes? A week? And to what or whom? To silence? Or mystery? Though sometimes a shivering sense of Belonging rises up, amid the icy rocks and creaking trees.

When we travel we are always looking out at the physical world with the *eye,* and in, at the self, at the *I.* This delicate, difficult braid of self and world, of both seeing and seeking, is for me at the heart of the writing process. But it's also at the heart of prayer. Seers and seekers.

Again, I think of the sweat lodge. And how I was always searching in the dark heat for some spiritual destination that I couldn't find. I used to wonder if the others in the circle were also seeking, or if they were already *present* in the song and drum, already a part of the *Belonging*. Seeking and seeing. Where does one end and the other begin? Do they ever converge?

Sometimes it feels like they do when I'm walking, and trying to listen to the rhythms of my own body—the legs, lungs, and heart of an animal moving across the earth. *Walk and you shall see. Seek, and you will not find* what you were looking for. So keep walking.

§

When I got back to the Abbey, the kneeling man was still out there fish-praying. Still no fish though. I had no desire to join him in the middle of the frozen lake, but I felt some sympathy, and connection, as that's what I was doing—waiting, praying, and a kind of fishing—for words, and a different kind of time. For what Thoreau once called, "the gospel according to this moment." The imperfect present.

I listened and looked for it, as I tramped from the lake up the hill, to the Abbey, for 5:00 prayers with the monks. Happy to be some place warm, I filed into the choir and sat down in one of the heavy oak choir stalls. There are four daily prayers in the liturgy of the hours at St. John's. But on the shelf in front of me were seven prayer books: seven little plastic blue binders, the kind with three-holes and silver rings. Which book? Morning, Midday, Evening, Book of Song, Feasts, Common, or Responses/Canticles? I chose Evening, and a thin, black-robed, 40-something monk behind me immediately came up and pulled out the Book of Song. "This is Mass 8," he said quietly, and opened the book to the Psalms for Monday, Week 1 in Ordinary Time.

When I still couldn't find the 8th Mass, I sort of came undone. I'm not sure why, or how, I jumped from my "gospel of this moment" meditations at the lake to that anxious, agitated "What am I doing here?" moment. Why was I more comfortable in the freezing forest sanctuary than in that toasty warm one? I preferred being outside to being an outsider. I again felt like a tourist. Like I was looking at rather than seeing. And why wouldn't I? Aside from not knowing which prayer book to use, I wasn't Catholic, didn't really *know* how to pray, or cross myself, or bless myself with holy water, or chant psalms melodically, or bow at the right times, or if I should take communion, or how time could be ordinary, or anything else.

That was when my guardian monk returned, opened the prayer book to Mass 8, the hymnal to page 82, and nodded toward the signboard on the wall which listed all the info for the day—the week, mass, song, and psalm. He knew I hadn't noticed it and smiled gently.

"Thank you," I said.

"You're welcome," he replied. But in his kind, calm eyes, I heard a third word. Or did I just want to hear it? I couldn't know for sure. Did it matter? Yes. Why couldn't I believe in it?

You're welcome *here*. Even if you don't know where you're going, or how you'll arrive. It was a word I didn't expect or know I'd been waiting for.

A Great Plenty

*Do we detect the reason why we also did not die on
the approach of spring?*
—Henry David Thoreau, JOURNAL VII (4/6/1856)

The soft spring rain felt like an invitation. So I waited and
watched.

As a crazed blue jay bullied a starling off our birdfeeder,
a coyote slinked through the prickly wall of buckthorn that
lines our yard, and stepped onto our wooden deck. He was
peering through the cracks between the boards—hunting the
pack of chipmunks who have turned the dark cavern below
into a new subdivision.

Was it the same coyote I surprised at our garbage can a
few days prior? Only eight feet away, and staring him down
through a large window in our family room, I still couldn't tell.
Even when I waved and tapped on the glass he ignored me,
indifferent, even defiant. Finally, he loped away.

A wild creature abruptly appearing in our suburban back-
yard conjured up a writer I've come to rely on over the years.
Thoreau, too, refused to be domesticated. I started rereading
him amid the cabin fever of the pandemic, and found his
musings on his two-year quarantine at Walden Pond newly

relevant. Maybe because he also lived through a pandemic—tuberculosis—which took his life at 44. "Only that traveling is good which reveals to me the value of home," he wrote, "and enables me to enjoy it better." Thoreau loudly proclaims the gospel of *now* over and over in *Walden*—that the present tense is not a cage but a gift, that solitude should inspire rather than mire.

During the Covid pandemic, such ideas have been useful. Most of us found some relief from physical isolation in Zoom-athons and social media, but that kind of presence only goes so far. Soon, the sad hum of anxiety began to drone 24/7 from our laptops and smart phones, and so we got reacquainted with the natural world, or with our partners, or ourselves, as we learned to travel at home, and reimagine time—to recover the arts of baking bread and reading books or simply walking.

Thoreau might call this new attentiveness—to place and people and presence—"a more deliberate life." Not a simpler life, but more meaning-filled. For some, it was the silver lining that still shimmers.

But the pandemic has caused more shadow than shimmer—enormous suffering and loss. Millions of people around the globe have perished, and hundreds of millions have lost their jobs or businesses.

I lost my mom during Covid. It was a year ago. Though 95, with a walker and waning memory, her death unleashed an emotional typhoon in me that was equal parts grief and gratitude. The waves are still breaking now, as I write and watch the rain, and think of her, and her deliberate life—the joy she found in the daily routines of life in a small town. Like Thoreau, she was frugal and stayed put. Unlike Thoreau, the family she created was her home.

I sensed her presence that morning, as the rain ticked on the roof, and a robin glided by with a beak full of wet grass, and flapped up to his mate in the crook of a silver maple. She was preening in the nest—adding and adjusting the twigs and leaves—getting ready. The birds had just returned to Northern Illinois from a winter feeding ground somewhere south. An internal geomagnetic compass allows them to *home* their way back to their nesting place each spring. For birds, home is both verb and noun—both journey and destination.

Oddly, I think it was for my Mom too. She was always *traveling home*, to her family. Though she had a different kind of compass, a different magnetic force—love—which she shared with anyone who could not find their way, including me, and my dad and three older brothers. Her needle always seemed to be pointing to others. I think it still is.

§

The care center where Mom lived, in St. Paul, Minnesota, was in quarantine the week that she died. It was March, 2020, with patches of green appearing through the melting snow, and Covid-19 sweeping across the Midwest, smothering the hope of spring. My brothers, Robin and Paul, who lived nearby, would have a nurse take a cell phone into Mom, so they could Face Time. They would explain to Mom about the pandemic, and why they couldn't come inside, and how they didn't know when the quarantine would end. Each day she'd forget, and they'd explain all over again.

The last time I called, from our home in Chicago, Mom didn't remember about the virus, or that the cafeteria was closed, or even where she was. "Everything is fine," she said, sounding weak. "Though I think I'm just about done with this job." She lived in the fog of dementia, but it often thinned, letting more light through.

"I just don't seem to get much done anymore," she continued. "You're 95," I said, "you don't have to get much done. Let people do stuff for you for a change." She chuckled at this. Then I asked what they had for dinner. She couldn't remember. "Oh, nothing fancy," she finally said. "But it was a great plenty."

A great plenty. The phrase, which Mom often used, stuck in my head, and still does now. For her, it meant "there is always enough." Though she often used it when there wasn't—like at a poorly attended church potluck or fundraiser. "We'll make do," she'd always say.

Like thousands of other elders who were isolated from their children and grandchildren due to the Covid virus, Mom lived through the Depression and Dust Bowl and Stock Market Crash and WWII, and other times when having *enough* was both gift and goal, a cause for gratitude. The Covid era has been such a time—a time of fear and loss, where we have struggled to imagine enough. Enough money or work or facemasks or Covid tests or vaccines, or *compassion* to make it through.

The word compassion literally means "to suffer with," and it's the quality I most admired in my mom. She knew it was what enabled the possibility of "a great plenty," of their being enough—for everyone, no matter the zip code. And that's the world she lived toward—in small ways, in a small Iowa town, but with great love.

At the time, I was thinking more about that town, Maquoketa, because we were amid the most critical and combative presidential campaign in my lifetime, and I disagreed with some of my Iowa friends that I grew up with. They supported Donald Trump and his wall and Muslim ban and the bashing of the press and his dog whistles to white supremacists. Some asked if I was a socialist, and others if I was still a Christian. My response was yes. So we ranted and vented on Facebook, returning to the sandbox of childhood, which, big surprise, was a waste of time. I still could not wrest away my friends' metal pails or shovels, nor they mine. But like many, I was sucked into a culture of either-or thinking—of constant reaction, and no reflection—which I still regret.

It was also the first presidential election that Mom—a lover of politics, and passionate Democrat—could not follow. Though given Covid and Trump and the media vitriol, it wasn't a bad one to miss. Mom liked face-to-face campaigning—hand squeezing and baby hugging at county fairs and diners and park pavilions. And since the Iowa Caucuses were the first Presidential testing ground, all the candidates always came there. You could actually meet them! One even slept over at our house (Sen. Paul Simon). Mom never really understood the internet or social media. She never sent an email or texted or owned a cell phone. Over the years, most of Mom's "news" came through the telephone, the radio, and four TV stations. Or through the various streams of small-town gossip, which pooled in the coffee shops and churches.

Mom watched her beloved *News Hour* on PBS for decades, but the last time I visited she couldn't follow it anymore. Then her eyesight grew cloudy, so she couldn't read the newspaper. The outside world was shrinking for her. Through the windows of her room, or the cafeteria, she watched the leaves and light changing, or she talked to her caretakers or her children. Her compassion still burned, but it was more personal, elemental—the glimmering embers of a dying fire.

The day after I talked with Mom on the phone, my brothers were notified that she was near the end. So they rushed to the care center, and in spite of Covid protocol, were buzzed in. Evading the wheelchairs, and frail bodies shuffling by, they hurried toward Mom's room, and the growing darkness. But they couldn't make it in time. Mom had just died, in the arms of her nurse, Gail, whose face was still streaked with tears when they arrived.

I later called to thank Gail for being there at such a sacred time when we could not. "It was a blessing to be with Dee," she said. This startled me. It was "a blessing" for Gail to risk her own life—on the front lines of the pandemic—to be with my mom?

Her voice, so clear and certain, filled me with gratitude. And since George Floyd was murdered nearby shortly thereafter, igniting demonstrations across the Twin Cities, the image in my mind's eye, of a middle-aged Black nurse, and her White, elderly patient, has grown more emotionally charged: Gail cradling Mom in her last moments, suffering with her to the end. The personal bridging with the political, in a world where bridges seem impossible.

Though my brothers and I video conferenced many times after Mom died, it was confusing to grieve alone, and to figure out what to do about a funeral. We didn't want a virtual funeral, and since Mom was cremated we kept pushing the date back, hoping more could attend. But the pandemic didn't wane. So that summer we finally had a grave side service in Iowa City, where Mom and Dad used to live, and where my brother, Ken, still does.

Nine masked people in a circle remembering and grieving and celebrating. It was so bright and hot that day that some of us broke out of our socially-distanced circle to step back into the cool shade of the oak trees that towered over the grave.

During my time to speak, I recalled one of several conversations I had with Mom about her fear of death. "I'm not too keen on it," she told me. "And I don't believe all of the 'pie in the sky' stuff." And then, after a pause: "But I do believe in God; that there's something more."

This prompted me to pull out "Let Evening Come,"[9] a poem by Jane Kenyon, which I read at my father's funeral, and suggested I could read at hers. The first stanza is: *Let the light of late afternoon/shine through chinks in the barn, moving/up the bales as the sun moves down.* The poem is full of images that call rural Nebraska to mind, where she and Dad grew up.

I noted that every stanza in the poem contains the word "Let." Not "The sun shines" but "**Let** the Sun shine." Not "Evening Comes," but "**Let** Evening Come." We talked about our fear and not knowing, and about God and the mystery of God's love. And if rather than having to know, we could just **Let** God handle it. **Let** evening come. **Let** yourself belong to Creation.

And then, in a moment of lucidity, Mom said, "I suppose that's the faith part." She put her hands over mine, offering love amidst her own cycles of worry. A little while later I rubbed some of her Jergen's lotion into those old hands—into her palms and the crooked fingers which used to play the piano so meticulously—and then, into the thin, dry skin on her forearms. As I did this, she closed her eyes, and let out a deep sigh. I could sense a ripple of happiness, or relief, or something, and then realized she was simply enjoying a rare moment of physical intimacy. "That feels good," she said.

"It's really hard to be old isn't it?" I asked a little while later.

"Yes, it is," she said, her eyes still closed.

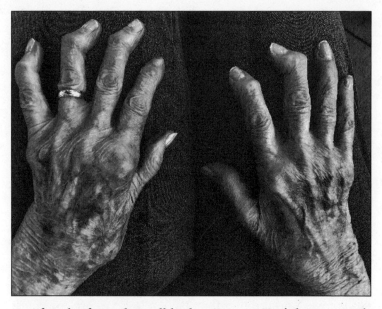

After the funeral we all had a picnic at Ken's house—with carry-out box lunches from the local co-op where Mom used to work. Since we were six feet apart, and outdoors, we removed our masks. The only way we could touch each other was through the love we could conjure with our words. Physical touch: we all felt the presence of its absence—the distance between us. And then, a couple of hours later, we drove home to our own Covid-infested cities.

During the next week, I sorted through some old photos and letters from Mom, which was a comfort. Especially one black and white shot of her swimming, which Rob took, and which I couldn't stop looking at. Rob had inspired my own love of black and white photography and printing when I was in high school. In the darkroom, I learned to frame the black and white image so that it would both limit and invite the beholder. A good photo, or painting, or essay—I finally figured out—feels both framed and frameless, both limited and limitless, which is what draws me to this one.

Mom loved to swim more than anyone I know. In this image, she is 75 years young and there are no boundaries or borders. The horizon merges with the sky—nothing but water and light, and my mom, paddling toward me. Moving out of the sun into shadow, from light into darkness, an image of death perhaps. But she looks at home in the water. You can see it in her eyes. And that she is not just swimming out of the light, but carrying it with her wherever she goes.

§

By noon the rain let up, so I stopped staring out the window, and gathered my things. Since it was the anniversary of Mom's death, I was driving to Sawyer, Michigan to scatter her ashes at Tower Hill, a church camp where we went as kids. And where Carol and I would later take our kids. Mom loved the place.

The trip from Glen Ellyn to Sawyer takes two hours. I don't think I would have made the drive if I hadn't also scattered my father's ashes in the river a few years prior. That day the current of the water carried away some of my grief, along with my dad—and some oak leaves, a few water striders, a turtle, and the bass and crappie we used to wait for and wonder about. I felt his death not just as separation, but as belonging.

When I arrived at Tower Hill I remembered: they tore all the cabins down a few years ago. But I found the site of Cabin 14, where we used to stay, sprinkled some ashes on the concrete foundation, and then walked back into the old-growth white pines, to "God's mailbox," in the middle of the forest. There passers-by could write and "post" a letter to God. Mom would have liked the last note someone had scrawled on a scrap of paper.

GOD,
Thakng you for the
anamals I bve you

I returned to the cabin site and then made the familiar twenty-minute walk, through the woods in the other direction, to Lake Michigan. As I followed the old path, I thought of Mom's floppy sun-bleached hat, and huge canvas bag full of half-used tubes of suntan lotion and magazines and diet books and bags of corn chips and granola bars, and how, when we reached the wooden bridge, we'd tramp down to the creek and walk the last quarter mile in the gurgling, sun-dappled water.

My memorial walk in the creek ended at the lake, and the stretch of beach where Mom loved to swim. So I kneeled down, and pulled out a handful of ash to scatter on the sand a few feet below. But a gust of wind abruptly sent the ash flying upward, into my face, and then blowing back down the beach. It tasted smokey and gritty, like when I clean out the fireplace. So I just swallowed, wiped the dust from my eyes, and tried again when the wind ebbed. This time I sprinkled the white ash closer to the ground. When the wave arrived, Mom swirled in the light for a few seconds, then was swept out into the deep, dissolving into everything.

Once More to the Lake, the Elephant, and the Weasel

Remembering is an act of spiritual meaning, pushing us against the unknown. Thinking back through time can be like reaching into the dark, murky water with no idea of what your hand will come across: a lovely shell or something with spines and venom. Remembering, like all matters spiritual, requires imagination, trust, and courage.
—Margaret Bendroth, THE SPIRITUAL PRACTICE
OF REMEMBERING

I used to think that getting through college required more grit and self-sufficiency when I was young than it does now. How about those summer jobs we had back in the day? Like riding my bicycle five miles each way on gravel roads—with brushes rattling in a roped-on plastic bucket—to paint an old farmhouse. Or spending the day ripping shingles off a two-story barn roof with a rusty spade, or walking beans, or baling hay, and always in 100-degree heat. Such jobs allowed me to earn a full year's tuition each summer ($900.00 in 1979). We were so frugal and such hard workers. So why are "kids today" going into such debt?

But such nostalgia is neither relevant nor accurate. And that's what my freshman comp students told me the one time I shared this perspective in class. One student reminded me that college costs had risen 1000% since I was in college, but the minimum wage had only doubled. Then others shared stories about their crazed and exhausting attempts to balance full-time work and full-time school, but always coming up short.

And the pandemic brought new challenges as well. My son, and his friends at college, all of whom contracted Covid-19, spent a year wondering if/when/how they would return for the next term. Many were 100% online while living at home. From their childhood bedrooms they viewed canned lectures or Zoomed into classes where there was no discussion—all while simultaneously snap-chatting and tweeting their equally disoriented friends, and wondering what their college degree would mean now, and what it would/n't lead to.

The spirals of insecurity and doubt prompted by the pandemic sent Gen Z's already record-setting anxiety and depression levels soaring. In spite of all the hi-tech apps and options for multi-modal communication, it may be the loneliest generation. In her latest book (*iGen*), psychologist Jean Twenge describes Gen Z as "…scared, maybe even terrified. They have come to adolescence in a time when their primary social activity is staring at a small rectangular screen that can like them or reject them."[10]

One thing the pandemic revealed is that while technology is an essential and powerful tool, it alone cannot *educate*— cannot give us the self-knowledge and courage we need to follow what we love, and to believe it will lead us where we need to go. Which is the same glorious and humbling challenge we all encounter in college, and beyond. I remember.

§

On a hot August day, in 1979, I moved from Maquoketa to Iowa City, and into Burge Hall, or "The Zoo," a dorm that housed 1000 freshmen at the University of Iowa. My "cage" was a 10 by 12-foot room, where I would live with two other bewildered teenagers. As my parents and I pulled boxes out of our car, I remember two songs drifting from the open windows of the dorms: "Imagine," by John Lennon, and "Lonesome Loser," by the Little River Band. That day, given my uncertainty, I identified more with the latter. The two films everyone was watching then were *Apocalypse Now*, a gruesome critique of the Vietnam war, and *Animal House*, a raunchy fraternity romp. Like many freshmen, my social life overwhelmed my social conscience, so I was in party mode. I would only be in class three hours a day, the sparkling *Saturday Night Fever* disco balls were spinning everywhere, and I was finally on my own.

But it took awhile to adjust to dorm life. In high school, I was a fairly big fish in a small farm pond. Not a privately stocked rainbow trout—not from the deep cultural waters of Chicago or Des Moines, like many on my dorm floor—but rougher, a carp, who didn't mind eating off the bottom. So the kids from suburban Chicago (where I now live) intimidated me. They spoke a different language. Most were "rushing" and "pledging a house," which I knew little about. And they had sports we didn't: tennis and swimming and soccer. They'd never heard of "Shop" class, or 4-H club, and had never detasseled corn or castrated pigs. They were sophisticated, and had more money and confidence than I did.

The first month of college was one long staggering party full of desire and confusion: *this* was college? But I wasn't alone. My roommates and I, and a few other guys down the hall, all happily bonded through our shared but unspoken sense of displacement. Every night at 6:30 PM the flipping whir of a helicopter, Alan Alda's familiar voice, and the laugh track from *M*A*S*H* seeped through our half-closed door. We all comfortably sprawled on the floor around our 10-inch TV screen for 30 minutes before heading to the all-you-can-eat cafeteria, and the steaming silver vats of mashed potatoes and chicken-fried steak and buttered carrots, which I loved. The only thing I liked more was the pop machine. I could drink four or five glasses of Coke or Pepsi and no one cared. The salad bar had been invented, but didn't interest me. In those days quantity mattered as much as quality. There was no obesity epidemic, or calorie postings, and a lot fewer choices. Two kinds of coffee: regular and decaf. No shade-grown Sumatra with chocolate notes. And, after dinner, two kinds of beer: regular and light. No hoppy IPAs with a tangerine finish.

There were no computers or smart phones. We plunked away on typewriters that had arms and bells. For mistakes: white-out and retyping. We snaked the phone cord under the door to get some privacy in the hallway when we called our parents "long-distance"—on Sunday after 5:00 PM, when rates were low. Given the forty cents per-minute rate, there was no time for chit-chat. The one serious conversation I remember that fall was regarding my first ever "C"—on a paper in World Politics. Mom: "Don't worry, you're just starting out. College isn't easy." Me: "Thanks, Mom. I agree." Dad: "I thought that was going to be your major. Will this affect your Pell Grant?" Me: "No, I'm an open major, so everything is fine." When I said "open" I could hear the smile in my mom's voice, and the concern in Dad's.

What else did we talk about in those brief Sunday evening conversations? I liked to bring up the news headlines (from World Politics, my favorite class, in spite of the "C"): Three Mile Island had exploded, the Soviets had invaded Afghanistan, the US-USSR arms race was escalating, and 47 American hostages still huddled in Iran, waiting. But the event that captured my imagination that fall was an astonishing coup in Nicaragua, where the Sandinistas, a band of young Marxist renegades, had overthrown the government of Anastasio Somoza, the US-backed dictator-president. I remember a *Time* magazine cover story with a photo spread. "*No Mas Imperi-*

alismo," said the sign hanging in the Managua Plaza after the Sandinista takeover.

Those classes and teachers awakened my social conscience, which began to direct my social life. The next year I joined the college-wide Nuclear Arms Freeze and the Central American Solidarity committees. For two years I wrote letters, attended dozens of meetings, gave a bunch of talks, and took all-night buses to Washington, DC, where we marched and chanted and visited congressmen and the Soviet and Nicaraguan Embassies. I still liked my academic work, but it seemed less important.

In the spring of my senior year, I asked an English professor I admired, Cleo Martin, what to do after I graduated. I'd been offered a high school teaching job in Washington, Iowa, a town much like the one I grew up in. But I was also accepted into a graduate program in nonfiction writing—the first of its kind. After a long discussion about balancing teaching and writing, and whether you could do both, Cleo said, "Listen to your heart." So I enrolled in the writing program—unprepared, unqualified, and oddly determined to write about the war in Nicaragua.

On the first day of my first class—"Advanced Expository Writing"—a know-it-all student from New York, a self-identified "working journalist," began jabbering about George Orwell's "rare ability to bridge fact and truth." I didn't know what the hell he was talking about. Since it actually *was* 1984, a discussion then arose about the modern relevance of the novel, which I pretended that I'd read. The whole first semester was like that—lots of pretending, and later tracking down everyone else's references to books and writers I'd never heard of. Thankfully, our teacher, Richard Lloyd Jones (Jix), was smart and kind, and expected the stark differences in our abilities and backgrounds.

In the next class session, with a thin stick of chalk, Jix scratched the word "essay" on the blackboard, and added the origin (*essai*) and root meanings: "trial" or "attempt." Then he said that the personal essay was the nonfiction equal of a short story. I was both startled and relieved, because for me, the word "essay" meant dry academic writing. But I loved short stories. So even amid the booky, beery haze of those first weeks of grad school, I soon became interested, and somehow hooked on the idea of the essay. Maybe because my life had begun to feel like one—like an odd, spiraling experiment.

In that course, we read twenty or so essays in an anthology. But three of them stuck with me. The first focused on family and memory (E. B. White), the second on neo-colonialism and culture crossing (George Orwell), and the third on nature and spirituality (Annie Dillard). All topics that would later become the focus of my own trials and attempts (including in this book).

Jix assigned the first two essays for contrast. One was quite political, looking mainly outward at the world, and the other deeply personal, looking more inward at the self. George Orwell's "Shooting an Elephant" (1921) *did* read like a short story:

a clear plot with an emotional climax. Orwell, a member of the Imperial Police in Burma, had to kill a huge elephant "solely to avoid looking a fool." Uneasy with his unearned authority, and confused by Burmese culture, he botched the killing, and the animal died a slow, excruciating death. The essay is a critique of British colonialism. Orwell was trapped: he detested the British Empire he represented, yet was also hated by the locals he was supposed to protect.

One line in the essay would later haunt me: "when the white man turns tyrant it is his own freedom that he destroys." In later years, I would find strands of Orwell's story in my own—in Nicaragua and Guatemala and the Philippines and other sites of US colonialism, where I would work and write and struggle to fit in, and to undo Euro-American privilege. Mostly I failed.

While Orwell's essay was fast-paced and political, E.B. White's "Once More to the Lake," (1941) was slow, intensely personal, and didn't read like a short story. When White was a kid, each summer his father took their family to a lake in Maine for vacation. The essay is about a nostalgic return trip he makes decades later to the same lake, with his own young son, who had never been there.

Some students in the class liked the piece, but others found White's endless memories and reflections self-absorbed. He kept imagining himself as his own father, and his boy as himself, a few decades earlier. "I began to sustain the illusion," he writes, "that he was I, and therefore, by simple transposition, that I was my father." Such middle-aged insights didn't connect with the younger students. I didn't love the essay, but I didn't mind it. Maybe just because I liked to fish.

But twenty years later White's story would become my own. And that line—"that he was I"—would return to me, when my son was born. So would the "simple transposition that I was my father," when my dad later died from Alzheimer's. These events revealed to me something White clearly knew: time *does* move faster as you age. It's not a delusion. When you're five years old, a single year is one fifth of your entire life. And there are two central events that have occurred: learning how to walk and to talk (and how to fall and to listen). But when you're 50, one year is one 50th of your life. You're still learning how to talk (less), and to listen (more), but there is a lot of other stuff to remember, and forget—college, marriage, children, broken bones and hearts, a leaking roof, a friend's death from cancer. Or maybe shooting an elephant or going fishing with your kid.

The third piece, Annie Dillard's "Living Like a Weasel," was more overtly philosophical than the other two. A nature essay by one of Thoreau's literary offspring, it explores the relationship between instinct and reason. I loved that Dillard's "wilderness" was not wild, but suburban, and that it was a weasel teaching the human animal how to live.

But Jix used the essay to teach a basic writing move: the "framing" of an arresting image or moment in order to both limit and invite the reader's attention, while introducing a theme. Dillard put a frame around a death match between an eagle and a weasel. But that didn't matter to me as much as the strategy. I needed help—some basic models for how to see and read my life like a writer. And now I had one: the camera. It was all about framing and focus and perspective. About inviting yet limiting the reader.

When I left that class I'd just begun to understand the chaos and beauty of the perpetual "trial" of the essay, of writing, of *seeing* a life. And I'd begun to get my head around a core idea that was likely self-evident to everyone else: out of the millions of moments and images that we perceive, and that constantly buzz through the wild circuitry of our brain, we can only ever retain and frame a few. That's what Jix was always getting at: What do you choose to see? Where are you focused? What few precious moments will you frame, and turn into art—into a handful of stories—that will *once more* come to stand for a life.

On Saving / Seeing the World

Do not be conformed to this world, but be trans-
formed by the renewal of your mind ...
-ROMANS 12:2 (ESV)

Last summer, our daughter, Abby, was reassigned by the mission board of our church to work in Managua, Nicaragua. She had her plane ticket and was getting prepared to go. She'd had to leave an assignment in San Cristobal, Mexico, due to Covid, and another position in Nogales, Mexico, due to security threats. Which was why it was disheartening when violence and political unrest broke out in Nicaragua, and the situation just kept getting worse. Nicaraguan President Daniel Ortega unleashed a brutal crackdown, jailed all of his opponents, and closed the country to journalists. So Abby had to shift gears once again, and take a different position—this time with Americorps in Oregon.

But her "almost" placement in Managua left me nostalgic, as I had spent time there when I was her age. Though not as skilled or experienced as Abby is, I had the same 20-some thing idealism: a longing to both see the world, and make it a little better. Oddly, Daniel Ortega was also the President in 1985-86 when I was there. But he was not the tyrant-dictator that he has since become. Rather, he was the head of a revolutionary government, which had just *overthrown* a dictator (Somoza), and was committed to lifting up the poor majority—through land redistribution and massive new education and healthcare programs. Ortega and the Sandinistas were then viewed as a prophetic, radical model for change by other poor, underdeveloped countries. The US, however, saw them as a Communist threat that needed to be squashed.

After my first year of grad school, as Ronald Reagan's war against the Sandinistas was heating up, I spent the summer in Managua. I wanted to "Experience the Revolution First Hand," like the brochure for my language school promised. Many Americans were going to Nicaragua then, to witness the covert war that our government was waging—and to report on it, to expose the lies. The stakes were much lower, because I couldn't be drafted, but the war in Nicaragua in the 1980s would become, for me, what Vietnam was for my older brothers in the 1960s: the public historical event as personal moral dilemma that requires you either take a position and do something, or stick your head back in your books. My "higher education" was just beginning.

At the time, I'd only been in an airplane twice, and never out of the US. So my arrival at Managua's Sandino International Airport was startling. Managua was not Maquoketa. As

I slouched and sweated in the 100 degree heat, some of the guards in their Sandinista greens would walk over and point their AK47s at me and the few other gringos in the airport. And then they'd walk away. Was this random? I had no idea. The immigration "line" was a sweaty swarm of frustration, with everyone pushing to get in front. Since it was my country waging a war against theirs, I didn't push. Outside, just beyond the customs gate, I could read a hand-printed sign on the chain link fence: "Yanquis Go Home."

The other problem was I couldn't understand their Spanish. It was not like in my classes back in Iowa City. No one seemed to pronounce things quite right. And they changed and dropped letters. *Vamos* was *bamo. Los dos* was *lo do. Las vidas* was *laz bida.* And everything seemed to run together. It was embarrassing. Why did the well-dressed man in front of me keep mentioning *dinero* (money) and offering me a taxi? He wasn't. He was asking me if I'd seen *Taxi Driver* and what I thought of Robert De Niro? The woman behind me wasn't saying my pain didn't matter: *"No vale la pena."* (The pain has no value.) Rather, the phrase was an idiom (I later learned) meaning "Don't worry about it."

My ride from the language school didn't show up, so I followed the "on your own" back-up instructions, and went looking for a bus stop. The #42 would take me to Barrio Riguerro and my host family. A dozen other people were already waiting there and found the Birkenstocked white guy—the *sandalista*[11]—with the bright blue L.L. Bean back-pack, an amusing distraction from the dusty heat.

Ten buses went by, but no #42. An hour or so later, I could see the 42 painted in red on a scrap of plywood propped in the windshield of an oncoming rusted yellow Bluebird School Bus. Jammed with passengers—more bodies squeezed in the aisle than sitting—a dozen arms were sticking out the windows because there was no room for them inside. A bunch of kids white-knuckled it on the outside, clinging to the thick chrome rear molding and luggage rack on top like refrigerator magnets.

I wedged my way in the door, stuck a wadded 10 Cordoba bill in the driver's hand, but was smashed back into the sweaty mass of humanity before I could get change. I fought to make a space for myself, but didn't go in too far, for fear I'd never get out. The old man sitting next to me gave a child a drink from a knotted baggie full of ice water. A woman behind me with a couple of live chickens in a burlap bag, accidentally jammed them into my back every time the bus stopped. When I turned around to see what was poking me, she smiled apologetically. I asked her how far to Barrio Riguero; she said she'd tell me when to get off.

As the bus weaved and hissed across the city, through acres and acres of wooden shacks and darting lizards and mangy dogs and blaring radios and rumbling wooden carts, it all began to blur together—like it didn't matter where you got off. There was always a vendor selling bananas or mangos, a pick-up baseball game nearby, and some kid in faded Sandinista greens squatting in the shade, waiting. All the stops looked the same to me.

"*El próximo! El próximo!* (The next one!)," the kind lady with the chickens finally shouted. The bus was off again with a hot carbonic hiss, so I started my frenzied squirm toward the door, four feet away. "*Con permiso. Con permiso.*" I mumbled as I pushed and writhed, hoping to reach the suction of the exit vacuum near the door and be spewed out at the next stop. Just as the kind lady yelled—"*Aquí! Aquí!*"—I was swept out of the bus by the river of bodies, into Barrio Riguerro, an enormous dirt-poor barrio, and Sandinista stronghold.

After a few wrong turns, I arrived at my home for the next month: a two-roomed cinder block and plywood house. My host mom, Dolores, and her teenage daughters, Johanna and Lesbia, were patient with my ignorance. Late, on that first night, the wind started blowing mangos from their tree onto our corrugated metal roof—Boom! Bang! Boom! Bang! I woke terrified, sure we were under attack. Dolores and the girls couldn't stop laughing about this. Nor about my later thinking that their dog's name was "Afuera!" ("Outside!") because they kept yelling at him to "Get out!" of the house. Nor about the electric pink blotches (Pepto Bismal) I heaved all over their patio one night (thanks to a parasite).

One day I walked across the Riguero plaza to find a crowd gathering around a makeshift plywood stage, behind which someone had strung up a banner: "*De Cara Al Pueblo.*" Then I looked up to see President Daniel Ortega, and Jaime Wheelock, the Minister of Agriculture, and their security detail, all walking straight toward me, then right by me, and up on the stage. The freaking President of the country and a cabinet member had just strolled into our barrio to "Face the People." I was stunned. Ortega gave a brief talk on "the state of the revolution," and "Reagan's covert war," and then opened it up for questions—about everything from the national literacy campaign to land redistribution.

Later that week, I used my press pass from *The Daily Iowan* to go out in a press pool to cover a Contra attack near Masaya with writers from the *New York Times* and *Washington Post*. A few days later I got into the government headquarters to interview Fr. Ernesto Cardenal, the renowned priest-poet, and Minister of Culture. Cardenal founded a church community of *campesino* artists on the Soletiname Islands in Lake Managua in the mid-seventies. The "primitivist" art from that community was known throughout Latin America, as was Cardenal's book, *The Gospel of Soletiname*, a kind of oral history of the Bible studies he led there. Inspired by these stirring conversations about faith and history, many in this *communidad de base* would later join the Sandinistas' guerrilla war against the Somoza regime.

In the interview he talked about a split in the Catholic Church and why Pope John Paul had denounced him, and why "Christian Socialist" was not a conflict in terms. Near the end he turned to writing, and the role of journalists, and left me with a bit of advice: "You don't have to save the world," he said. "You just have to see it." Or maybe he said, "You cannot see the world, so why do you think you can save it?" I was not confident in my translation. I chose the one that made sense to me. In part because that was the tone of his other comments in the interview: outsiders cannot understand everything that's going on here. Just because someone is silent doesn't mean they don't have anything to say. Listen longer. Later, I realized he was also alluding to my failures to listen, and my unearned privileges as a US journalist.

The next week Dolores and the girls took me to their church in Riguerro: *La Iglesia de Los Ángeles.* I had read about it, and their priest, Padre Uriel Molina, who had worked closely with the Sandinistas in the overthrow of Somoza. He knew Daniel Ortega well, and had grown up with Tomás Borge, who was one of the founders of the *Frente Sandinista Liberación Nacional* (FSLN). Some of his students at *La Universidad de Centro America* would become central players in the new FSLN government.

Like Ernesto Cardenal, Padre Uriel was known throughout Central America as a chief proponent of "*la teología de la liberación*" (liberation theology), which took Central America by storm in the seventies, upending the traditional hierarchical Catholic Church, which had supported some brutal dictator-puppets—including three Somozas, who ruled Nicaragua from 1932 until 1979. Even after the Sandinistas took power, the Catholic hierarchy forbade priests from giving Sandinista soldiers communion, or even a Christian funeral and burial.

I later interviewed Padre Uriel. The time with him was unsettling and inspiring. Uriel's fierce commitment to the "least of these," to his *barrio*, was contagious. "We too are a chosen people," he said, referencing the Exodus story. "We too had to escape decades of bondage and hunger." Long before the "historical Jesus" movement was popular, Molina and his base communities were doing contextual theology, and reading the Bible through the lens of their own experience.

"Christ the savior did not only die for our sins. He was tortured and crucified because he preached liberation for the poor," he explained. "So we are less interested in theology than in theo-praxis. In acting as Christians we become Christians. Half of our national budget goes to fight your country's war against us. We need that money for food and healthcare and schools. We are called to resist the violence."

It was all so simple, and overwhelming. Padre Uriel was *enacting* the radical faith of the Beatitudes, and the Sermon on the Mount, and all those other Bible verses I had read so many times. There were of course other prophetic leaders I admired—King and Gandhi and Dorothy Day and Bonhoeffer and more—but I had never met any of them.

In mid-August I returned to Iowa City, full of political passion, but promptly found a different kind. I fell in love with a bright and beautiful psychology student, who, thankfully, was also interested in me. One night I invited her over to my tiny basement apartment. I had splurged for a gallon of Carlo Rossi chardonnay ($4.00), and a large bag of animal crackers. Soon writing and the war in Nicaragua didn't seem so important. But then it did again, because it was to Carol. After an intense four-month courtship, we decided to go to Nicaragua at the end of the spring term. She wanted to see the revolution first-hand too, and I needed more material. So in mid-May we got our plane tickets, loaded our backpacks, and headed south.

In the meantime, the war had intensified. The US Congress had just approved 100 million dollars in aid for the US-backed Contras, thinking a new offensive might overthrow the Sandinistas. Thus, the Sandinistas were certain a US ground attack was imminent. And if one believed *The Barricada* or the other Nicaraguan papers, it was coming within days. On the bus from the airport to Dolores' home, we saw hundreds of tanks encircling the city center—pointing outward—one tank every 200 yards. Should we be worried? Who could we believe? We didn't have access to radio or television, and had to wait in line for an hour to use a public telephone. And even then, the connections were dicey. The newspapers were all we had.

A few days later a notice about a Sandinista rally in Chinandega was scratched on the "events" chalkboard in the foreign press headquarters. The Defense Minister, Humberto Ortega (Daniel's brother), was going to speak. So the next morning we took a taxi to the Chinandega bus station. The rally was on a large cooperative farm a few miles out of town, and by the time we arrived a crowd of 500 people had gathered. Ninety percent were Sandinista soldiers, and something about the way they were holding their rifles and the intensity of Ortega's speech worried me. He was clearly angry, but the speakers were too distorted and scratchy for us to translate his words.

And then, with the political tension rising, the tired, sweaty soldiers began marching and chanting *"Aquí, Allá, un Yanqui Morirá.*" At first we didn't get it. And then suddenly we did: "Here, there, a Yankee will die." Startled, I looked around at the sea of green soldiers, all toting AK47s, and then at Carol, with one of those "What in the hell are we doing here?" looks. As the only Yankees in attendance we were uneasy—but also amused by the irony. Was it a romanticized solidarity or the public spectacle of our silence that prompted us to join in the self-condemning chant? I'm still not sure after all these years.

And I'm not sure how we decided to get married in Managua a couple of weeks later. We discussed the implications and risks, but not for too long. We just followed our hearts. Perhaps the wild dream of our love had somehow absorbed the creative passion of the Nicaraguan experiment. So a few days

before we left for the States, we met with Padre Uriel in his office and arranged to be married in his chapel the next day. He didn't mind that we weren't Catholic, or that we'd only been dating for five months. That night we washed our best clothes in a large metal pan—Carol's cotton sun dress, my jeans and the one shirt with a collar. They dried stiff in the wind by morning.

I remember how the cool shadows of the empty chapel quenched the scorching heat of the street outside the open window. Padre Uriel had cut a few stems of Bougainvillea and brought them for Carol—a *campesino's* bouquet he called it. There was no music. Padre Uriel read the traditional passage from Corinthians, and then one from Paul's letters to the Romans: "Do not be conformed by this world but be transformed by the renewal of your mind." After the vows, he grabbed both of our hands in his: "The gift of your love offers you both solace and courage," he said. "You'll need both." Then Carol and I kissed, and the ceremony was over—in like 15 minutes. We signed the marriage certificate, thanked Uriel, said our goodbyes, and walked off into the dusty heat—thankful, and a little bewildered: we were married.

§

During the same time I was in Nicaragua, there was another revolution going on against another US-supported dictator on the other side of the world. In February, 1986, the non-violent People Power Revolution forced the president of the Philippines, Ferdinand Marcos (and wife Imelda) to flee to exile in

Hawaii. After his departure, Cory Aquino, wife of slain congressman Ninoy Aquino, was immediately thrust into power. I knew about Marcos' overthrow, but little about the history of the Philippines until we moved there a few years later, to teach in a small college, as missionary "co-workers."

The Rain Makes
the Roof Sing

The Filipino people have had the misfortune of being "liberated" four times during their entire history. First came the Spaniards who "liberated" them from the "enslavement of the devil," next came the Americans who liberated them from Spanish oppression, then the Japanese who "liberated" them from American imperialism, then the Americans again who liberated them from the Japanese Fascists. After every "liberation" they found their country inhabited by foreign "benefactors."
—Renato Constantino, THE PHILIPPINES: A PAST REVISITED[12]

Upon first emerging from the baggage claim area at Ninoy Aquino International Airport in Manila, Carol and I waded through the heavy air toward a mirage of curious, gleaming faces peering through the chain link fence. I was abruptly reminded of the first time I arrived in Managua—on the other side of the world—a few years earlier, where a bunch of kids were also hanging on a chain link fence, the airport their only entertainment. This parallel between the Philippines and Nicaragua would return a month later when I handed my Filipino writing students a stack of five by seven black and white photos of vendors and farmers that I had taken in some unnamed country. I asked them to describe their response to the images, and to try and identify the country and the culture. I wanted to discuss writing as "moment-framing," but also to see what they could discern about the context from the pictures. To my surprise, some of my students mistook my photos of Nicaragua and Nicaraguans for the Philippines and Filipinos. This led to a discussion about what "culture" is—about language, cuisine, religion, history—and how some parts can be desecrated by colonialism, while others can't. It was a conversation that never really ended during our time there.

After a three-hour bus trip from Manila south to Batangas, we boarded a rusty, overloaded ferry for Mindoro, an island to the south. We bobbed and weaved through the choppy

South China Sea for four hours before arriving in Calapan, the Mindoro port. There we met Modesto, a community organizer who worked in Mamalao, a remote village. He would hike with us there the next day, and serve as our guide. As we boarded a tricycle (motorcycle with sidecar) to get into town, he explained that the people of Mindoro were known as the *Mangyans*, and that the twelve families who lived in Mamalao belonged to a tribal group within the Mangyans, known as the *Irayans*.

Modesto found us a plate of rice and squid in the market for dinner, and then we walked to his friend's house, where Carol and I would spend the night. About midnight we woke to the high-pitched squeaks and grinding teeth of a pack of large rats feeding on a rice sack a few feet from my head. I finally got the nerve to pull the sack into the next room. The rats followed. I turned the fan on high to help drown out the menacing squeaks and chewing. It didn't help. I lay awake watching the seconds and minutes blink by on my digital wristwatch.

Eventually, morning came. After some leftover rice and squid for breakfast, we loaded our backpacks. Unsure of what to expect, and clinging to the illusion of self-sufficiency, I packed a mini-pharmacy, mosquito netting, and three changes of clothes.

The week in Mamalao was part of an ongoing orientation program for new missionaries, the last of our week-long "exposures" to educate us about the diversity of Philippine culture before beginning our two-year teaching assignment at a small college in Laoag, a town in the Ilocos region of Luzon.

During the People Power Movement, in the late eighties, Cory Aquino's government kicked all the foreign missionaries out. They later allowed them back as "coworkers," who were required to learn the language, study the culture, and live similarly to Filipino counterparts—the same salary, and no cars or telephones, or positions of leadership. So we signed up to teach at a little college, where they needed faculty. I would teach English, and Carol psychology and religion.

§

It was typhoon season. So when I realized we had left our rain ponchos in Manila, I went looking for Modesto. He had just returned from the market with a large bag of rice, a small jar of instant coffee, and six cans of sardines. He also had bought some huge plastic bags, which worked better than my poncho, slipping easily over both my body and backpack. How had he known?

Not wanting to sleep with the rats again, Carol and I were glad to leave for Mamalao. But we also knew that Modesto's friends had given us the best bed in the house and the only fan. They had thumbtacked a sheet over the open doorway for privacy. The other four people who lived there had all piled into a small room above us. They had offered complete strangers the very best they had. Yet I was unable to trust their concept of safety, and instead yielded to fear and worry.

A driver pulled up in a muddy, rusted jeep. We climbed in and headed for the foothills. When the road ended, we crawled out and began the day-long hike up the mountain to the village.

Modesto had packed only a towel with a few clothes wrapped inside. He stuffed this in a plastic bag with a small, aluminum rice pot. He also carried all the food up the mountain.

. An hour into the hike the rains came. In minutes the steep path became a muddy, brown water slide which Modesto miraculously negotiated in his rubber flip-flops. I slogged and slipped after him in my mud-packed Nike running shoes, pausing every few minutes to pick off the leeches which suddenly appeared on my ankles, arms, and every leaf or vine I grasped for support.

We finally reached the village and stopped in a bamboo chapel to rest. The rain was booming on the metal roof. We had to yell to hear each other. Modesto pointed to the roof.

"White man's noise," he said, smiling.

Thinking he meant "white noise," I nodded. The hammering rain on the metal was deafening and buried any sounds from the jungle. The diversity of insects, birds, monkeys, and other animals was all drowned out by the white noise. There was, though, something about the all-consuming noise that was comforting, that created a kind of placelessness and timelessness which allowed me to turn inward for a moment, to escape the reality of my isolation, my "exposure," my not fitting in.

Modesto later explained that a white missionary had bought the chapel roof as a gift when he visited the community several years ago, which was why the twelve Irayan families who lived in Mamalao called the engulfing sound of rain on steel "White man's noise." The White man had left a noisy roof. Given the choice, the Iraya would not have retrieved the large sheets of steel from the port and carried them into the woods. They would have spent the money differently—probably for rice seedlings to plant on the terraces they had just started on the mountain. Roofs were something they could easily construct themselves from bamboo or other local fronds. Thatched roofs didn't last as long as the metal roofs, of course, but they were cooler and more easily repaired. Not to mention quieter.

The rain continued. That night, while lying next to Modesto on the floor of our bamboo hut, I considered the drawbacks of the metal roof. A good-hearted outsider had unknowingly misread the culture in an attempt to help. I knew I would do the same thing.

After the orientation was over we moved north—from Manila to Laoag. The day after we arrived I went for a walk to familiarize myself with the city. Most of the teenagers or adults I passed turned to stare at me. Eventually, some would smile and call out "Hi Joe!" or "Americano!" Some of the smaller children would point and say *"puraw"* ("white") to their friends, to be sure they didn't miss me. One boy on a bicycle who was craning back to get a better look at the newly arrived oddity he had just passed, rode smack into a *balete* tree. Two other little kids walked straight into a *bougainvillea* bush. Scratched and stunned, they crawled out of the flowered bramble on all fours, laughing. Not being used to all of the attention, I became equally clumsy, nearly hanging myself on low slung clothes lines or electric wires, cutting my head on the corners of vendors' shacks, and slipping in fresh dog doo, which always seemed to be strategically laid right in the middle of the street. I felt very tall and very white.

Seeking a quiet and inconspicuous place, I started walking toward the cathedral bell tower, which jutted above a line of tin roofs near the river. It seemed close. But after several blocks of meandering and a few wrong turns, I found myself in the middle of the Sunday market: two square blocks of patiently swarming men and women with woven bamboo or plastic shopping bags. They deftly avoided stalled fruit carts and mountains of pineapples or mangos, as they perused hundreds of makeshift wooden stalls in search of a particular item or price. I wandered into the dusty chaos and was swallowed whole, submerged in a writhing labyrinth of color and smell: sizzling chicken feet and bloated sausages skewered on bam-

boo, huge kettles of boiled duck embryos, plastic buckets full of large black beetles, wooden crates overflowing with okra, eggplant, and seaweed, bananas dangling everywhere in yellow, green, and red clusters, dozens of greasy-hot, bright orange *empanadas* dripping cool on metal racks, and a long row of shiny, steel pails sloshing with silvery milkfish, snails, blue crabs, and shrimp. Nearby a woman hacked off large chunks of a thirty-pound bluefin tuna with a *bolo* (machete), weighed them, and put them in a baggy for her customers.

Feeling overwhelmed and disoriented, I wandered into a kind of tunnel, formed by two long walls of bulging 100 pound sacks of rice, piled high on either side. This emptied into the tobacco section—a row of women who rolled, bagged, and smoked cigars while waiting for a sale. As I walked by I felt a touch on my leg, and I turned back to see an old woman smiling up at me. Squatting with her knees up by her shoulders, she extended to me what looked like a freshly rolled tobacco leaf, tied at either end with a light string. Then she removed a similar cigar from her own mouth so she could speak. I was astonished. The tip of the cigar that had been inside her mouth was bright orange. She had been smoking with the lit end inside her mouth! She laughed at my surprise.

"Oh, oh....yes, yes," she said, with an amused smile. "We like better this way."

"You try. Free," she said.

I tried to match her minimal English with my minimal Ilokano (the regional language).

"*Diak kayat ti tobacco, ngem agiaminak.*" ("I don't like tobacco, but thank you.") She laughed—not expecting Ilokano to come out of my mouth—and motioned for me to sit down. I squatted down in a position similar to hers. She asked me my name and where I was from. I reciprocated. "I am Ima," she said. After two more short attempts at conversation, and several minutes of just squatting there, she laid a bunch of tiny bananas in my hand.

I was relieved, and confused. Did this Ima, this tough-skinned, fire-eating old woman understand what I was feeling? Just before I rose up out of my squat to leave, she patted me on the knee, looked at me, and nodded reassuringly.

So I waded back into the market, ducking ropes and bamboo poles as I drifted in a sea of arms and legs and dickering voices. Later, I found myself washed up by the cathedral, my original destination.

§

A month later the first typhoon of the season hit Laoag. Typhoon Kadiang arrived abruptly, taking down tree limbs and power lines, blowing rain through the screens, cooling the house. When we lost electricity I lit a small candle and anchored it on a metal lid with a few drops of hot wax. I sat at my desk in the teetering light and tried to read my English Composition students' responses to their first in-class writing assignment. I asked them to write a one paragraph response to the question: *What is love?* Not wanting to waste paper, groups of four students shared one 8-1/2 by 11 sheet, carefully tearing it into quarters. Most wrote only a sentence or two.

Due to the wind I couldn't keep all of the wrinkled scraps of love weighted down, the candle lit, or the rain out, so I moved to another room, choosing hot and windless over inconvenient but cool. But without the breeze to distract me, the incessant pounding of rain on metal was barely tolerable. I was consumed by the barrage of sound which refused to diminish, and then, after nearly an hour, amazingly, got louder.

None of the students who lived with us seemed to notice the torrent of rain, or seemed to mind it. Mhae, though she surely couldn't hear herself, was playing her guitar and singing with Lita. I watched them for a moment, but couldn't tell what song they were mouthing. Narissa was studying intensely with a trio of thick candles set up around her. She had positioned them so the flames danced wildly in the wind, but somehow were never extinguished. The shifting light and sinister shadows didn't seem to affect her concentration. Eden was outside on the porch talking to her boyfriend under the overhang. Carol was reading Jane Smiley's *A Thousand Acres*—a novel about a farm family in Iowa—with a dim flashlight. Iowa, the place I'll always come from. My corn and cows and October frosts had been replaced by rice and water buffalo and typhoons. I felt like one of Smiley's characters. I too was going nuts.

"*Love is like the mango—ripe, sweet, everywhere. Everyone eat the mango. Everyone love.*"

"*Love is patient and gentle—like slow bubbling rice.*"

"*Love is feeling I have with family that we both know.*"

"*I love Yang, our carabao. We depend for each other.*"

*"My mother nursing her bebe—up all night. Love is
what that is."*

The students' responses pulled me out of my frustration.
I was intrigued by the variety. When I gave the same assignment at home, at the college where I taught in Chicago, my
students, who were more adept at English, wrote less concrete
responses. Most were close to this: "Love is a strong emotional feeling or bond which a person has for another person or
thing." The whole idea of this introductory exercise is to distinguish between writing that tells or explains and writing that
shows or reveals, to move from vague, abstract concepts to
concrete imagery. It was interesting how the Filipino students
seemed to more readily give examples, to show love rather
than attempt to explain it. I wondered if there were any cultural implications.

*"Caring is love. How do we care? When they dyna-
mite fish in my place they are not caring about the
coral. Now there are no fish. No coral or shell. Now
there is no love."*

*"My brothers and I work together. We love to work
together. We love each other. We trust each other."*

*"Love is not always so easy. Sometime I am hard up
for love. Two boys courting me. They play the guitar
for me, but I don't think it is love."*

"Love is banal."

Love is "banal"? This response, one of the shortest and least
concrete, confused me. In part because I hadn't heard the word

since we arrived in the Philippines. Love is dull, common, and ordinary? I wondered if I was missing something. Could she mean that love doesn't need to be extravagant or overly complicated, that it's necessary and habitual? I didn't think so, at least from the little I knew about "love" in Philippine culture. "Banal" would seem to describe what love is not.

I asked Lita for help.

"'Banal' means 'sacred' or 'holy,'" she explained.

"It does? I've never heard that definition."

"That's because you don't speak Tagalog," she smiled.

I told her that there was also a word in English spelled "b-a-n-a-l." She had never heard of it.

Just then Lita hurried off toward the door. "You're not going out are you?" I asked. "No, no, someone is tapping at the gate." How in the heck did she hear that? How did she distinguish that faint metallic tapping from the roar of the storm?

It was a neighbor. I'd forgotten her name again. She wanted to borrow a candle. Lita had some extras and went to get them. The woman, who was sopping wet despite her best efforts with her umbrella, sat down near me in the flickering light and smiled. "Adu!" ("A lot!"), she said, referring to the rain, trying to be cordial. "Demasiado," (Too much,") I replied. She laughed. It didn't seem to bother her that we were yelling. "No, no," She shouted, "Mayat!" ("It's good!") "What?" I asked, reverting to English. She looked confused. "What? What is good?" I asked again. "The rain. The rain is good," she said, now in English. She pointed to the metal roof. "Listen," she said. The rain was actually beginning to let up—a machine-gun instead of a jackhammer overhead. "The roof sings," she said smiling again. "Huh? It what?" I asked. "Listen," she said. "The rain makes the roof sing." She looked at me like we shared a secret. I desperately wished we did. I understood what the sentence meant, but not her deep, knowing gaze. I wondered if she knew that my affirmative nod was in ignorance.

And that's when it finally hit me. This was the same "white noise" I had heard in the jungle a month earlier. But now it was bugging *me*—the White guy—instead of the locals. Later that week I asked some of my students about this. Laoag was not the jungles of Mindoro, they told me. Metal roofs were preferred in Laoag. Sheet metal was readily available, reasonably priced, durable, and easy to transport from Manila. Thatched roofs were less durable, often required patching, and few Ilokanos knew how to construct them. So they were rarely used. In short, Irayan culture in Mamalao was different from Ilokano culture in Laoag. One student, Pablo, quickly put this in perspective after class one morning: "There are 120 different languages spoken in the Philippines," he said. "If you cross a mountain range, or take a boat to a different island, you'll probably find a different language, and a different culture."

A little while later, Lita returned with the candles. The woman said "Agiamanak," ("Thanks"), and headed back out into the downpour.

I kept listening, waiting for the watery rhythms and melodies to reveal themselves. But nothing came. That was all I needed. I had found a specific inanimate target for my general frustration: the rain on the roof. But then the neighbor lady came along and exonerated it. The rain made the roof sing! I wondered why she was so happy, and what kind of song or voice she heard. And I wondered if I would ever hear the intricacy of Philippine culture above the constant hum of my own.

The next afternoon the rain dwindled to a soft drum for an hour or so. But two days of downpour had deadened my hearing. The depth of the quiet was overwhelming. I found myself yelling, still competing with the imagined sound of rain on metal. Narissa laughed when I spoke too loudly, joking about my needing a hearing aid.

I pulled out another folder of student writing. Just to vary things I asked this class (more than half were religion majors) to respond to the question "What is God?"

"God is not here. I not believe now because of suffering much."

"God is hope."

"God walks in muddy fields. He plants seedlings—new life."

"God is what always there is."

"God is rice. God is rain."

God is rain? Was somebody trying to tell me something? That night after supper the rain completely stopped. It was replaced by the frogs in the flooded banana grove near our house. They were not as loud as the rain, but close. I lay awake sweating and listening to the great burping swamp of noise, the slippery green, cold-blooded chorus, swelling then waning, swelling then waning, seemingly without reason.

I paid closer attention and just kept listening. Soon I began to notice that this was not one huge croaking wave of sound, but a sea of specific croaks with different rhythms, tones, tunes—perpetually interrupting each other. Yet despite the seeming entropy, it was clear they were all singing one song. Amid the cacophony, there was an odd, unexpected harmony, a collection of sounds which were at once chaotic and healing. Harmony—sounds that sound good together precisely because they're different. That night something changed. I was beginning to hear things.

The next morning the typhoon was raging again. Classes were canceled. I slid the capiz shell windows closed and pulled out some more student writing.

"God is always, but not one thing."

"God the source of all things is. God the creator and redeemer."

"God? Seguro adda. Diak ammo. But I think yes."

"God is Espiritu (spirit)—everywhere. I never wonder no God is here."

The last two responses confused me. In Ilokano *adda* means "is present," and *diak ammo* means "I don't know." Since there are a lot of Spanish words in Ilokano, I assumed that *seguro* meant the same thing it did in Spanish: "certain." But that didn't make sense: "God is certainly here. I don't know." Then I remembered that some of the Spanish words were spelled the same but had taken on different meanings during the colonization process as they were integrated into Ilokano. "Seguro" in Ilokano means "maybe," not "certain" as it does in Spanish. I wondered about the historical implications of that.

Did the early Filipinos respond "seguro," ("certainly") in the unquestioning affirmative to their Spanish masters, but actually mean or think "maybe" in their unwillingness to yield or acquiesce, in their longing for other options? Now the phrase made sense. "Maybe God is here. I don't know, but I think yes."

The next sentence also confused me: "I never wonder no God is here." More multi-lingual confusion. I marveled at how my students balanced the regional language (Ilokano), the national language (Filipino), the language of instruction (English), and often an indigenous language. But with my limited Ilokano and minimal Filipino, I was often confused by the frequent language hopping in their writing. Here one word caused the problem—"no." "No" means "if" in Ilokano. Again I wondered about the colonization process, about Spanish or American conquistadors saying "no" and Ilokanos learning to hear an "if," to hear possibility in denial or condemnation, to see a crack of light seeping beneath a locked door. "I never wonder if God is here." I found myself longing for this student's certainty. But I was thinking more about belief in myself than in God. I wanted to believe that I could acculturate in an isolated rice farming community in the Philippines. And I wanted to believe that I should be teaching English, "the language of the colonizer," or "the language of money," as one of my students once characterized it while explaining why English should be relegated to a foreign language.

I put the papers down and listened to the rain, wanting to hear an "if" beyond all of the "no's" I had accumulated while trying to live in a radically different culture, while awkwardly groping toward integration and acceptance. I started thinking about the English and Filipino definitions of "banal." Somehow the bilingual irony seemed related to the "if" I was looking for. How does one learn to see and hear the "banal" (Filipino) in the "banal" (English)? How does one learn to find meaning and value in what at first appears to be meaningless?

My students and friends were trying to help me understand. In their immense patience, they were trying to teach me to live in the present tense, to pay compassionate attention to the world, to listen and see carefully enough to discern the possibility of the extraordinary in the seemingly ordinary, to hear the sacred music in the off-centered wooden rumble of two wagon wheels, and a slow, cloppity ox, pulling a rice farmer and his son back to their land, back to that raw green rectangle of life. They were teaching me that "love is like a mango," that "God is rain," that frogs can croak in harmony, that a "maybe" can be better than a "yes," and that an "if" is not always so far from a "no." They were teaching me about the writing process, but also about the difficult process of crossing cultures.

That afternoon the typhoon finally waned. The torrents of rain and wind faded as the storm blew down the coast. People took the opportunity to get out of their homes. They emerged from behind bamboo gates to see how the typhoon had left their world. Dozens of mangoes, still too green to bruise, had prematurely blown to soft thuds in the leafy soil around their wooden houses. Children collected them in plastic buckets. Then they began to pick up the wet green tangle of bougainvillea vines and broken acacia limbs. Finally, they swept up the tattered banana leaves with short stiff brooms made from the ribs of a palm frond. The dust pan was a large cracker tin cut away on one end and wired to a pole.

A vendor walked by balancing a long pole on the back of his neck with two silver pails at either end. "Mami! Mami!," he called, peddling noodles. As the streets began to drain, horse drawn carriages gradually reappeared. They taxied people to the market or on some other long-delayed errand. A neighbor rolled up her pantlegs and stretched a rice sack over her head for protection as she waded across the still-flooded banana grove. Three green coconuts, a hubcap, and a freshly drowned cat floated by her on the way. She stepped over the open sewer and up onto the street on her way to the corner *Sari Sari* store for some eggs.

I kept listening. The rain became light and easy. It softly tapped gentle, corrugated rhythms. The tapping evolved into a pinging, and I began to detect tinny, dented melodies. They unrolled themselves like banana leaves in the sun, their immense hidden beauty slowly revealing itself without warning or effort. An hour later, I started grading papers, but still found myself listening to the roof, and searching for the quiet, elusive voice of the rain.

The Future
Behind Us

History is like a person rowing a rowboat. With his back to the front of the boat, to the future, the rower is always moving the boat forward, while intently watching his wake in an enormous sea—constantly considering where he has been. He faces the past while moving into the future. Where he has been guides where he will go. As the rower remembers, he moves forward.[13]

Several years after Carol and I returned from the Philippines, I stumbled across a bunch of photos from the Philippine American War on the Library of Congress website. One got my attention.

Taken in 1899, a regiment of US soldiers is gathered around a Gatling gun in Manila. I recognized this weapon—a forerunner of the machine gun—because it is a revised version of the Hotchkiss gun, which was used by the US military to massacre more than 200 Lakota people in Wounded Knee, South Dakota on December 21, 1890. The US army called it The *Battle* of Wounded Knee, suggesting the murdered Lakota were "battling" back rather than being mowed down by the rapid fire artillery guns. This is evident on the sign marking

the actual site of the tragic event: twenty years ago the word "Massacre" was painted on a piece of wood and nailed over the word "Battle," finally correcting the lie.

Since I had studied and taught that tragic event in my classes for many years, the picture of the Gatling gun in Manila startled me. I had somehow missed the fact that the last adversary some of these soldiers had faced—before their deployment to the Philippines—was that band of Lakota at Wounded Knee, who had resisted being rounded up and imprisoned on a reservation. I'd also overlooked how both events were misnamed in order to demonize the "enemy." The US military and the press did not call it the Philippine American War, but "The Philippine Insurrection"—as if the Filipinos were to blame for fighting for their own independence from their supposed liberator (the US).

When I showed this photo and others like it to my dad, he told me that his uncle, Chester Chamberlain, had fought in both the Spanish-American and Philippine-American wars. This news surprised me, as did Dad's having researched the topic at the public library in Northfield, Minnesota, a town near where the Chamberlains had lived.

It turns out that 22-year-old Chester joined Company E of the 13th Minnesota Volunteer Brigade and sailed to the Philippines in 1898 (a month-long journey). While there, he wrote letters home to his family and friends, which were published in *The Northfield Leader*. Dad gave me copies of these letters. I cringed as I read them. The first excerpt below describes the period after US and Filipino forces had defeated the Spanish under the command of George Dewey. This was when Filipinos were beginning to recognize that the US was not there to defend them after all, but to colonize them.

Nov. 19, 1898

Manila, Philippine Islands

...things are getting exciting now. No one is allowed to carry a weapon except the soldiers. I and another fellow were searching a lot of them we met on the street when I noticed a native slip out of a joint and slip along the street. I immediately ordered him to halt, but he didn't pay attention, so I brought my gun down to a ready. If he hadn't stopped I would've killed him. Our blood is to the boiling pitch now and

any native or Spaniard that makes a false move is a
dead man. We make 25 to 50 arrests a day.

Well, Thanksgiving Day will soon be here and
we expect a big time. Our regiment invites the
California regiment for a dinner in Frisco. We will
have turkey, geese, ducks, chicken, sweet potatoes,
banana fritters, oranges, several kinds of pie, fried
cakes, sauce, jelly, cake, ice cream, tea, coffee, and
chocolate, liquor, and other articles too numerous
to mention. This will be tapped off with music. How
is that for Thanksgiving in a heathen country?

My great-uncle equating the enemy, the Spaniards, with the "natives," reveals how the US was not fighting *with* or even *for* Filipinos in the Spanish American War, but asserting itself as a global military power. In the December, 1898, Treaty of Paris, the US negotiated a pay-off of the Spanish government to end the war, acquiring Guam, Puerto Rico, and the Philippines as US "possessions" for twenty million dollars. (Cuba was awarded independence.) In the months that followed, Commodore Dewey and the McKinley Administration reneged on their unofficial promise of post-war Philippine independence, and refused to recognize President Emilio Aguinaldo's newly established Philippine government. Claiming altruistic motives, the US chose to retain the islands as a "protectorate."

President McKinley called this policy "benevolent assimilation." The US would civilize its "little brown brothers" with American educational, governmental, and economic models—and with Protestant religion. But first, given the massive Philippine resistance to her so-called protector, it would do it with military force. Though the Philippine-American War officially lasted only three years (1899-1902) an estimated 300,000 Filipino soldiers and civilians were killed, along with 5,000 US soldiers.

My great-uncle reflected upon his experience in this war in an interview after he returned to Minnesota.

> *August 5, 1899*
>
> *Chester Chamberlain, newly returned home from service in the Philippines, believes the Filipinos can be subdued, but that it will be a good-sized job for an army of 50,000 men.*
>
> *"Their tactics are such," he says, "that it is hard to get an open or decisive engagement, as they fight from cover and then retreat. Our campaign plan while I was there was not very aggressive, but more to show the Filipinos that our men could go where they pleased on the island and at the same time conduct civilized warfare. But that kind of fighting is lost on the Filipinos, as they are treacherous and cruel."[14]*

I wish this history didn't matter—Chamberlain's white privilege and his dehumanization of Filipinos—and didn't lead clearly back to me. But it does. The Protestant missionaries, who came just a year after Chester Chamberlain, fervently lobbied President McKinley to retain the Philippines as new "conversion territory" rather than support Philippine independence. At the same time, dozens of other English teachers were arriving on the St. Thomas steamer in Manila Bay, intending to "civilize" the "treacherous and cruel" inhabitants of our new protectorate with raw ambition and boxes of English primers.

A similar process of "civilizing the natives" was going on in the US at the same time. Hundreds of Native American children from the many reservations were rounded up and sent to Christian boarding schools, where they cut their hair, put them in standard issue uniforms, and violently enforced an English-only language policy. The idea was to completely erase any signs of indigenous culture. The iconic philosophy of these schools—"Kill the Indian and save the man"—is tied to one of their founders, Richard Pratt. Later investigations also revealed that hundreds of Native children in these schools were raped by priests, other clergy, and church workers during this era. Many were killed.

And, while I find this brutal history tragic, it was and still is a part of my ethnic heritage and privilege. No matter how I tried to present myself, I could not undo what I *re-presented* as a white American in the Philippines. The same was true many years later when I returned to another site of Euro-American conquest: the Pine Ridge Indian Reservation in South Dakota.

Lost and Found
in the Holy Land

*Wherever we went, the soldiers came to kill us, and it
was all our own country. It was ours already when the
Wasichus made the treaty with Red Cloud, that said it
would be ours is long as grass should grow and water
flow. That was only eight winters before, and they were
chasing us now because we remembered and they forgot.*
—Nicolas Black Elk, BLACK ELK SPEAKS

The public bathrooms along Interstate 90 in South Dakota are
marked by thirty-foot high teepees made from cement pillars.
They remind you that you are in "Indian Country." A state plan-
ner somewhere probably thought they would trigger nostalgic
visions of Sitting Bull or Crazy Horse in tourists on their way
across the barren table of grassland to visit Mount Rushmore.

But driving further west, the strategy becomes more clear.
Most of the roadside billboards—marketing everything from
fast food to amusement parks to real estate—feature iconic images from Plains Indians culture: teepees, buffalo, the
medicine wheel, drum circles. Presumably, these images of
the Lakota Sioux people can spark a quite marketable curiosity in visitors like me, a curiosity that anthropologist Renato

Rosaldo once called "imperialist nostalgia": an odd, romantic longing for the culture that my ancestors nearly destroyed.[15]

I first recognized this feeling in myself many years ago, when I was invited to attend a Sun Dance on the Pine Ridge Indian Reservation—the central religious ceremony of the Lakota. My expectations didn't align with what I experienced those few days on the Pine Ridge: the dancers were all recovering alcoholics, the sweat lodges were covered with carpet remnants rather than buffalo hides, the sacred cottonwood tree was retrieved in a flatbed truck rather than on horseback, the eagle feathers were purchased rather than gathered, the drummers and singers used tinny microphones and cheap amplifiers that echoed with feedback, many of the dancers slept in nylon dome tents instead of teepees, and so on. I had still imagined a "traditional" Indian—as if tradition didn't evolve.

This mindset is just one way a middle-class white guy deals with his heritage—the near genocide of Native American people, and the theft of their land. And while I'm not directly *responsible* for that debacle, as a privileged beneficiary, and as a writer, I am *accountable*—able to give an account, of any "truth" I can find. That was partly why I was on my way back to the Pine Ridge—to listen for the stories that were not told, for some new truth.

Another reason, though, was to visit an old mentor: Francis White Lance, a Lakota medicine man. I would soon bring a group of college students to the Pine Ridge and Francis had agreed to mentor them as well, so I wanted to reconnect with him. Francis and I first met 25 years prior, when I was in grad school in Chicago and took a field study course: "Lakota-Christian Dialogue." Like Nicholas Black Elk, the renowned Lakota shaman from the Pine Ridge, Francis had also studied both traditions—with Gilbert Yellow Hawk, a Lakota medicine man, and at an Episcopalian seminary in Chicago.

The dialogue course met in Francis' small HUD-designed house. In the first session someone asked him how the Lakota viewed all the *Wasi'chus* (white people) who kept coming to the Pine Ridge to help and study them. "Most of us hate white people, and with good reason," Francis said. Then, as our discomfort bubbled up, he broke into a smile. "But don't worry, I might forgive you." This tension—between a bunch of well-meaning grad students, who sought to study Lakota culture, and our ancestors, who nearly destroyed it—was always there. It still is.

§

An hour later, I pulled off the interstate and into one of the cement teepee rest stops to use the bathroom. The parking lot was bustling with young families. Most of the cars had out-of-state plates. And it was June, so I presumed they were on vacation and on their way to the number one tourist attraction in the state: Mount Rushmore. The granite sculpture of the four presidents—each of whose head is 60 feet high—has been a tourist bonanza ever since it was completed in 1941. The sculptor, Gutzon Borglum, a brash, arrogant engineer (and member of the Ku Klux Klan), spent 14 years on the project, describing his work as "the first of our great memorials to the Anglo-Saxon."

The problem, of course, is that Mount Rushmore was sculpted in the heart of the Black Hills, an island of rock and trees about 120 miles long by 50 miles wide, which is the Holy Land of the Lakota people—the physical and spiritual heart of their culture. Long before the mountain was blasted and hammered into the four "white fathers," and renamed after a New York businessman (Charles Rushmore), the Lakota had a name for it: "Six Grandfathers" (the six sacred directions/spirits). So the sculpture still feels like an insult to them. Medicine man John Lame Deer put it this way: "they could just as well have carved this mountain into a huge cavalry boot standing on a dead Indian."

As I made my way to the men's room, a dozen or so kids and their tired parents roamed the rest stop. A mom told her sweaty, fidgeting son that it was still a long way to Mount Rushmore and their hotel.

"But they'll have a pool, won't they?"

"Yes, I checked," the mother said.

The boy was sucking on a dripping cherry popsicle. Behind him was a concrete relief of Rushmore artfully set in the brick wall. Beneath the sculpture it read "Great Faces, Great Places," the motto of the South Dakota Tourism Bureau. When the boy spun and started rubbing a sticky hand all over President Lincoln's pensive face, his mom went ballistic, grabbed his other hand and yanked him out the door.

I climbed back into my car, pulled onto the interstate and merged into traffic, but felt uneasy. Here's the thing: I knew I was an outsider, but did I qualify as a tourist? I had a nice camera, a beautiful laminated map, a shiny new rental car, and that uneasy sense of not belonging there. So there would seem to be little question.

Some writers call themselves "travelers" just to set themselves apart from the tourists, from the sightseers, the *site* seers. "Travelers don't know where they're going. Tourists don't know where they've been," writes Paul Theroux. Theroux also seems to see writing and travel as detours of intention, and as a constant process of discovery. Amid such journeys there is a creative tension: between the person and the place, between the culture you came from, and the one you are entering.

An hour later I swerved off of I-90 onto Highway 73, heading south into the reservation. The desolate two-lane blacktop—with its sharp dips and turns through grassy sunlit hills and dark valleys—felt more like a wagon trail than a modern highway. In the next 70 miles there were no McDonald's or Shell Stations or Red Roof Inns, or any place else to eat or pee or rest. In that 90 minutes I passed four cars, five antelope, two prairie dog towns, a large herd of cattle, three red-tailed hawks perched on various fence posts, and a lone person on foot. Walking along the dirt shoulder on the other side of the road, the Lakota man was tall, with dark shoulder-length hair, and was making emphatic gestures with his hands and talking to himself.

Troubled about his well-being—there was *nothing* within an hour's drive—I pulled off, made a U turn and stopped to offer him a ride somewhere. But he was smiling and calm, not at all worried or distressed, and waved me off. I drove on and watched his strolling, muted soliloquy in my rear-view mirror, until he disappeared into the vast, green hills. I couldn't imagine where he was headed, but the irony of my gesture, and of his calmness, was not lost on me: I was the one who didn't know where I was going.

As I snaked my way through the countryside toward Allen (population 400), where Francis lives, I wasn't looking for stereotypic snapshots of poverty, but I saw some: the tiny government-furnished house with a couple of abandoned cars and children in the front yard. One of the cars near the road—a rusted-out Mercury Marquis—had been completely stuffed with trash, with crumpled cereal boxes and beer cans. Something slimy—maybe fruit rinds—smeared the back window. A mile later two men were passed out on an old mattress laid out on the dirt driveway next to their trailer.[16]

The Pine Ridge is a hard place to live. Roughly the size of the state of Connecticut, it is the second-largest reservation in the United States and contains the nation's poorest counties. The statistics from recent studies are startling. The average life expectancy, 59 for men and 62 for women, is the lowest in the US and comparable to sub-Saharan Africa. The estimated rate of unemployment is the same as the rate of alcoholism: about 80%. The rate of tuberculosis is 800% higher than the national average, the rate of cervical cancer 500% higher. The high school drop-out rate: more than 50%. Forty percent of the homes on the reservation have no electricity, 60% lack a telephone.[17]

I looked up to see a road sign: **Pine Ridge 2**. It was two miles to the *town* of Pine Ridge. I pulled out the map. I'd somehow missed the turn-off for Allen. Another detour. But I had wanted to visit Pine Ridge and its ugly sister city anyway. White Clay, Nebraska, is one mile from Pine Ridge—barely off the reservation and over the state line. With just 12 residents, it wasn't really a town. But since alcohol was illegal on the reservation, White Clay had a booming economy at the time. Its four liquor stores combined sold 12,000 cans of beer and malt liquor each day.

Alcohol is at the heart of the social and economic problems that plague the Lakota—from domestic violence to diabetes to unemployment to suicide.[18]

I drove the mile into White Clay, and parked in a gravel lot at the end of the main street. I needed a picture of the liquor stores for a talk I was going to give at my college. Clusters of drunk men and women sprawled and slumped near the entrances of three of the stores. I had heard some of their stories on a prior visit—sad, predictable tales of violence and addiction.

I intentionally chose the one store without any people in front and pointed my camera. As I focused, a large Lakota man appeared in my lens—jogging toward me. It was hot— 90 degrees—and he wasn't wearing a shirt or shoes. Then he abruptly put his hand over my lens and grabbed my camera, yanking the strap tight against the back of my neck to pull me closer.

"Got to pay for pictures," he said, dropping the camera back against my chest.

I explained that I was only taking a picture of the liquor store, and not of any people. This distinction didn't matter to him. I should have known that.

"Five bucks for pictures," he said.

Then his friend came jogging toward us from across the road. Maybe 50, and wearing a dirty leather vest, he was smaller. He stepped up close to me, his chest a foot from mine.

"We're from the Crazy Horse band," he said.

I knew that Crazy Horse had never had his picture taken, but I had no idea what to say. The guy was drunk and hard to read. My non-response pissed him off.

"And we don't like pictures," he continued. "So give me some fucking money."

As I reached for my billfold in my back pocket to see if I had a few dollars to defuse the tension, he slipped his right hand under his opposite arm and pulled out a shiny black handgun, a 9MM Glock.

"Okay, I'll give you whatever I have," I said, praying he'd keep the polished barrel aimed down at my legs. He waited while I looked.

"All I have is twenty dollars."

This was when he pointed the barrel up, a few inches from my heart, and smiled. His teeth were dark and broken. Overwhelmed by fear, and the stench of vodka, I closed my eyes. Was this the end? What had I done wrong? I thought of my family.

"Please," I said opening my eyes. "Please don't." He gently tapped the gun barrel on my chest, smiled, took the twenty dollar bill from my trembling hand, and then slid the gun back under his arm. At this, his friend patted him on the shoulder, and chuckled. They walked back across the street and into the liquor store.

I hurried back to my car, climbed in, hit the auto lock. Shivering, I sat back in the seat and took a deep breath. What had just happened? My camera had reinforced the absurdity of my white skin (i.e. money) and marked me as the worst kind of tourist: the idiot kind, who wants a few shots of the natives to go with his shots of Mt. Rushmore to prove to his friends back home that he isn't a tourist. The kind who *looks* but can't *see.* The kind who doesn't know that he still represents the Cavalry coming over the hill. And that for those on the other side of the lens, the camera is still dangerous—a weapon which frames and dehumanizes.

When my racing heart had calmed, I pulled onto the road and headed back to South Dakota and Pine Ridge. There were two large signs on the state line. The first one I'd seen before—the Mount Rushmore drawing with the motto "Great Faces Great Places." But I hadn't noticed the other one.

A prisoner of war camp? Isn't that a bit far-fetched? The wars are long over. Though the reservation does at times seem like an unending internment, a prison of dependency. The story is long past and quite present: after the whites' systematic slaughter of the buffalo, and a century of broken treaties and land grabs, the US government finally convinced the remaining bands of Lakota-Sioux to come into the various forts and surrender their guns and land for good. Their reward: regular rations of beef, flour, oil, and sugar. Survival. In 1877, with his band of 900 followers starving, Crazy Horse finally surrendered at nearby Fort Robinson, Nebraska, where he was taken into custody and bayonetted by a US soldier. Chief Big Foot and his band of 300 were the last to surrender, in 1890. That didn't go well either.

Fifteen minutes later, still on my way to Francis White Lance's home, I passed by the small hill where Big Foot's band had camped—the Wounded Knee massacre site. From the gravel road below, I spotted a white woman, a tourist I presumed, sitting cross legged with her head down. Her back was up against the chain link fence which marks the mass grave of the 250 Lakota slaughtered there by the cavalry with Hotchkiss Guns. The woman seemed to be meditating or praying. Then she stood up and began taking pictures of the gravesite with her phone. Just as I had done on a prior trip.

After a few gravel road tangents I finally found the village of Allen, and the American Horse School, where Francis White Lance taught Lakota language and culture, and his wife, Suzanne, was an administrator. They had a small trailer behind the school. I knocked on the door several times before Suzanne came. Entering, I immediately remembered something Francis once told me: two things are always running in a Lakota home—the coffeepot and the television. A movie played on a large nearby flat screen—a wild chase scene. I didn't recognize the gun-wielding strong man—not Chuck Norris or Vin Diesel.

"Do you want some coffee?" Suzanne asked as she pulled up a chair for me. "Or something to eat?" In the next week I heard her ask that question over and over of all the neighbors and friends who constantly streamed in and out of their trailer. Both in their late fifties, with two grown children, Francis and Suzanne recently adopted two kids whose cocaine-addicted parents were imprisoned. Mandy, a two-year-old girl, was sick and crying. Curt, who is 5, was dressed in a camouflage uniform like a soldier from Desert Storm. He was firing a yellow, plastic battery-operated AK47 at me. It sounded real, which unnerved me. He's a nice kid, though hyperactive, since he was born with his mom's cocaine addiction. "He's already been in rehab, so he won't have to go when he's an adult," Francis later joked, the edgy humor a balm for a deeper pain.

So with the TV blaring, the baby crying, and Curt shooting at us, I tried to talk with Francis, who wasn't the least bit distracted. We drank Coke and ate bologna and white bread sandwiches while I asked him about his family. He pulled out some letters and what looked like a beat-up Olympic medal from a cardboard box on the bookshelf. It was the silver medallion given to his great grandfather, John White Lance, in 1868, as one of the signers of the Fort Laramie Treaty.

"The treaty gave us the Black Hills and the Powder Horn and a lot of other land, along with hunting rights," Francis explained. "But a few years later President Grant sent Custer into the Black Hills with an "exploratory" battalion. And they found what they were looking for—gold. Whites poured into the Black Hills to mine the gold, ignoring the treaty. Crazy Horse and Sitting Bull and others fought back. But Grant sent in more troops, who took the Black Hills back by force."

It took me a second to digest the history, and that I was holding the actual medal from the treaty signing 140 years ago. Francis talked about the event as if it happened last month.

"*He Sapa* (the Black Hills) is the Holy Land of the Lakota," Francis continued. "It is oracle and altar. It talks to you. All you have to do is listen. That treaty should be honored. We still want our land back."

I wondered if this were really possible: "How could the government give back land they no longer own or control?"

"In 1980 we won a lawsuit related to the treaty. And the Supreme Court voted with us," Francis explained. "President Carter and Congress offered us 106 million dollars to compensate for the theft of the Black Hills. That's supposed to be the value of the land in 1877, plus a hundred years of interest. But we didn't take it, because we don't want the money. The land is sacred. Money isn't."

That 106 million dollars set aside in 1980 has since swollen to two billion dollars and is now in a federal trust fund. A few years ago, some Lakota Sioux filed a legal suit to recover that money so they might divide it up and use it to meet basic needs. But the tribal leadership rejected this option, and is still holding out for a return of the land. They continue to assert that the land is not for sale, and that to take the money would bless the theft.[19]

I wanted to ask Francis some follow-up questions, but before I could, little Curt, who had been watching TV, suddenly wheeled and opened fire again with his battery-operated AK47. I took this as a sign. I'd imposed enough on Francis and Suzanne for one day, and Curt needed their attention. So I stuffed my digital recorder and camera in my canvas bag and said I needed to leave. On my way out the door Francis invited me to return at dusk for an *Inipi*, a sweat lodge. I thanked him, and got in my car. Meant for purification and prayer, the *Inipi* is the most common of the seven Lakota ceremonies. It often involves just family and friends. So I drove off to my motel feeling grateful to be invited again.

When I arrived back at Francis' place that evening, he and his friend—Ray Takes War Bonnet, a drummer and singer I'd met before—were tending the fire just outside the sweat lodge. A mound of large volcanic rocks glowed in the center of the flames. Then Dave and Tiger arrived, two young men who grew up nearby. I remembered Tiger from when he was a kid and the fire-keeper at a Sun Dance. But he had since begun training to be a medicine man with Francis. At the time Dave was a US soldier and was home on a two-week leave from

Afghanistan to visit his wife and baby daughter. He had a lot to pray about.

A half-hour later Tiger said the rocks were ready. He would run the sweat. So we put on our shorts and pulled off our shirts. Then Suzanne and two friends came out of the house in tee shirts and shorts and wrapped in towels. The lodge would be full.

I've been in many sweats over the years, but I'm always a bit afraid. It's a different kind of prayer: not dry, cool words rising from the mind in a bright ornate, oaken chapel, but water rising from the flesh, steam rising from rock, smoke from fire, and air from lungs in the hot, dark womb of the earth. Prayer not as human separation from nature, but as a raw physical convergence with it. The most common phrase spoken in Lakota ceremonies is *Mitakuye oyas'in.* "I am related to all that is."

The lodge was twelve feet in diameter and made of canvas remnants stretched over a red willow frame. It was low and wide; the roof peaked at five feet. After Tiger, Francis, and Ray had crawled inside, and had everything prepared, they told us to enter. We each said "*mitakuye oyas'in*" and creeped in on all fours. The dirt floor was hard and damp. We wriggled in until we were all crouched tightly together around the empty fire pit; legs against torsos, our bodies folded into thirds. Then the fire keeper outside lifted grapefruit-sized white-hot rocks from the fire with a pitchfork, threaded them through the open flap door hole, and dropped them in the pit, the holy center. Tiger arranged them with a deer antler, prayed, and sprinkled sweet grass and cedar shavings on them.

When the fourteen smoking, glimmering rocks were all arranged—a foot or less from our bare toes—the fire keeper outside closed the flap. The lodge was hot, the glowing rocks beautiful and frightening. I was dripping and trying to pray, but it was getting harder to breathe. Tiger sang prayers for the ancestors. His low, clear voice—my only compass in the darkness—seemed to point everywhere. Then he ladled water from the metal bucket onto the rocks and a cloud of steam rose from their sizzle. I kept breathing and trying to let go of my fear, to pray, to belong to the circle, to listen. I remembered what Francis told me when we were undressing: "The heat breaks down the ego and opens you to the spirit."

Feeling more lost than found, I tried to focus on this line, on the word *open*, until I fell adrift in the rising spiral of Tiger's song, and in the heartbeat of Ray's drum. That's when Dave started to pray—a prayer of gratitude for time with his family amid his tour in Afghanistan. The sad courage in his voice startled me back to the present, back to the circle. His words seemed to hover in the dark heat until they belonged to everyone.

Then Tiger began a new song, and sloshed more water on to the iridescent rocks. And in the mingle of light and darkness, the rocks cried out. Their soft hissing arms of steam lifted heavy waves of heat that pulled me back into their wordless prayer, back to the water and fire, back to the earth, back to the Wild, and to what I call God.

It was not until much later—when Tiger asked the fire keeper to open the door flap—that I recognized what a comfort the darkness had become, and how far I had traveled without arriving. Amid that soft flood of dusky light, our shining, crouching bodies reappeared in the smoky haze.

The sweat was over. So we got down on all fours and followed Francis and Tiger through the opening. "*Mitakuye oyasin*," we each said, before crawling out. Thankful and relieved, I pulled on my jeans and shirt and joked with Francis and the others while the moon brightened behind us.

The next day, I had to return home to Chicago. So I said my good-byes, packed my bags and headed east. That morning, cruising along I-90, into the endless reach of the Great Plains, the vast sweep of the barren land and the empty sky seemed to swallow up my ant-like car. I hummed toward the horizon at 80 miles per hour, but against all that space, felt like I was barely moving. It was desolate. Where were all the billboards I had noticed on my way west? The tours were all in the other direction. Tumbleweeds drifted across the road. And as I watched the turkey vultures rock and drift high above me, scanning the earth for food, I could not remember a time when I had ever felt so small, nor so deeply connected to the whole.

A Map to Somewhere

The way of a canoe is the way of the wilderness,
and of a freedom almost forgotten.
—Sigurd F. Olson, THE SINGING WILDERNESS

I have made two other trips to Quetico Provincial Park in Canada since taking Bennett a few years ago. The last trip was with my brothers. The two oldest, Robin and Paul, have gone to the Quetico every summer for 30+ years. But their sacred tradition was interrupted by Covid-19, as Canada closed its borders. When they reopened a year later, Rob and Paul made a reservation, and invited Ken and me to come along.

Though the four of us have gone together many times, on recent trips, I've begun to feel a bit apprehensive. I love fishing and paddling and exploring the wilderness, but I'm the youngest brother. Rob and Paul are in their early '70s; Ken and I in our early '60s. The sad fact is I struggle to keep up with the old guys. It's not embarrassing, just humbling. They're tougher, want to go farther, paddle and fish longer, come rain or shine. They started going to the Quetico originally because the Boundary Waters Canoe Area—which is closer to their homes in St. Paul—has three times as many visitors, meaning more fishing pressure. And with all those people, it just feels less *wild*.

Speaking of wild: one thing I used to love about the Quetico was that we pulled our drinking water right out of the lakes. No need to boil or filter if we took water from deep locations and avoided beaver dams. No one ever got sick there. Until my sister-in-law contracted giardia last year. Now such infections have become more common. So, for the first time, we brought a water filter. The other difference on this trip was the wildfires—the worst in fifty years. The Boundary Waters Canoe Area had just been closed down. This made me nervous, but I repressed that fear, among others, and we all met in St. Paul, like always, packed up our gear and food, and tied on the canoes.

The night before we left the Ontario Park Service closed the Quetico due to fires. This was the first time that had happened. Rob and Paul were surprised but undaunted by the news. My thought was: "There are raging wildfires so widespread and dangerous that they have closed both the BWCA and the Quetico. Might we consider going elsewhere? There are some nice rivers nearby…" Kendall was thinking the same thing, but neither of us said anything. In the meantime, Rob had talked with Jean, a Quetico ranger he knew at the station in Atikokan, which was near our put-in. Jean had suggested an alternative route—in a provincial park adjacent to the Quetico. This area had not yet been closed.

The next day, when we arrived in International Falls, there was *no one* crossing into Canada. Usually, there's a long line of cars with canoes strapped on, and it takes an hour or two to get through. Though we all noted we'd made it through in record time, no one mentioned why: the freaking fires! When we arrived in Atikokan, to talk with Jean, the smell of smoke was overwhelming, and a gray haze hung on the distant horizon. Ken and I were not exactly gung-ho at this point.

In the past, whenever we discussed what route to take and how many miles we'd cover, I would always suggest that we canoe for several hours (4-5 miles) on day one, set up a base camp, explore and fish the area for the whole week, and then canoe out. This allowed for plenty of fishing time, for slower mornings—more coffee and contemplation—and maybe an afternoon nap in the hammock.

I didn't really expect them to listen to my suggestions, since I was the youngest and least experienced, and they always did all of the work. They organized all of the food and gear and we used their canoes and packs. But, on the last two trips they had acquiesced, and gone with the base camp model. And they seemed to enjoy it. So I thought maybe they were mellowing, and had my fingers crossed.

But the fire-dodging route that Jean had planned for us sounded like boot camp with boats. She got out a map and made a few Xs—marking the put-in, eleven portages, and the take-out spot. We would paddle through several lakes, which were connected by the Turtle River (which looked more like a lake). The whole trip was forty miles. And we'd have to break and set up camp each day. "This is a nice paddle," she said, "you can do it in 4-5 days, 8-10 miles per day." Rob and Paul nodded in agreement. But I knew that Jean was out of my league. I could maybe do half of what she proposed, if we didn't get smoked out first.

Since no one else asked about the fires, I did. Then Jean turned on her computer monitor to show us a live fire map, which glowed in different shades of red and orange depending on the intensity of the fire. The route she had suggested was not on fire, but there were some close by. Nevertheless, she assured us it was safe, and we all thanked her for helping us out.

When we got outside the ranger station, Rob and Paul knew that Ken and I were still unsure about the trip. "She's a seasoned ranger, Tom. If you can't trust her, who are you going to trust?" Rob said. He had a point, and she seemed kind and wise, but I wasn't sure I trusted *anyone*. Then we all discussed and approved the route she suggested. Though it's not like there were other options. And there was no way I was going to be remembered as the brother who bailed.

"Besides," Rob added finally, "Who knows how long this place will be around?" "Or how long *we'll* be around," Paul chimed in. How do you argue with that? And then, like always, Rob swept us up into his stubborn optimism and can-do attitude. Before I knew it we were standing in the parking lot jabbering about lures and who would catch the biggest lake trout, and telling stories from past trips. "I used to spend more time unhooking Dad's snags than fishing," Rob laughed. This got me thinking about the time Dad hooked a fish already on our stringer, and was convinced he had a huge northern. As we piled back into our cars, Kendall started whistling the theme from *The Bridge on the River Kwai*.

The first couple of days were hard and good. It was warm and sunny and we rarely smelled smoke. We canoed most of the day, set up camp at night, broke it in the morning, and just kept moving. We didn't fish much, so there were few fish to eat. We couldn't have any fires—my favorite part of camping—so that nightly pleasure was out. But we swam at dusk and sat out under the stars drinking single-malt Scotch out of plastic coffee cups and talking. Often about our portages, which were frequent and tough. "Rock climbing with canoes," Rob called it.

And yet the passage of time those days was wondrously slow and physical. Time and timelessness seemed like the same thing. Minutes were measured by our muscles and paddles and the wind and sun. Seconds by the haunting burble of a distant loon, or the rowdy gush of water over a rocky stream bed. Even the sweaty return walks during a portage—back through the woods to retrieve the remaining gear—felt calming and restorative. I didn't need my meditation apps. One afternoon, on the opposite shore, we saw a bull moose with a huge rack, wading in the lake. We all looked at each other and then went silent for a few seconds. A prayer of attention.

The first few nights at the campsite we kept mulling over what to do about our water supply, and thirst. The filter didn't work, so we had to boil. But given all the paddling, we were always thirsty, and never boiled enough. Finally tiring of the nagging thirst, we started drinking out of the lakes again. "It's never caused me any trouble," Rob said. But there had been a drought, and these lakes were not as deep as in the Quetico. Some looked more brown than blue. Perhaps it was just tannins, but we didn't know for sure. On one warm day, out in the middle of a huge lake, Paul dipped his bottle in and took a big drink. A few minutes later I noticed I could see the bottom. It was four feet deep.

On the third day, storm clouds started to circle, and we began to wonder where we were on the two maps we had brought. We weren't exactly lost, just uncertain about our location. And though Jean had marked all the portages on the little 8-1/2 by 11-inch map she gave us, we struggled to find them on the shoreline, and to recognize the various inlets and islands. We had a larger map of the area, which helped, but didn't resolve the problem. My brothers had never been on these lakes, nor on the Turtle River, so we could not rely on their topographic memories. The other problem was that neither map was waterproof. The patches of blue and green on Jean's map had run together, blurring into some new country that no one had yet discovered. The other map was also soaked and disintegrating and hard to read. No one ever brought a compass on these expeditions for some reason, so we couldn't determine direction except by the sun. We brought our cell phones along to take pictures, but it was too remote for any service or Wi-Fi. We didn't have GPS to tell us where we were, a compass to point us is in the right direction, nor a map to show the route to our destination. We were taking the long way home, but not by choice.

Later that afternoon, while drifting in a cove, with Paul again combing over the maps, trying to figure out where the heck we were, I decided to hit the maps icon on my iPhone—just for the hell of it. And lo and behold, after several seconds, a picture began to digitally appear—some patches of blue and then green. What was happening? And then, I recognized one of the shapes, and the outline of the Turtle River (Lake). And then the blue dot appeared. That was me! I knew where we were! Or the phone did. How was GPS working? It didn't on my brothers' phones. I had no idea.

No one seemed appropriately impressed by my discovery. Paul remained hunched over the water-drenched maps in the other canoe. "No," I said. "I mean it. It's *working*! I know where we are." I handed the phone to Paul on the end of my paddle. "O.K. I see where we are," he said. The iPhone map DID show us where we were, but nothing was labeled. So it still wasn't easy. We had to match up the digital blue and green shapes with the parallel land and water forms on the water-soaked map. And I only had 12% battery charge left on the phone, so we couldn't spend much time confirming our best guesses. As soon as we located ourselves I turned the phone off.

That night, while lying in my sleeping bag, I pondered the day's events. How ironic it seemed, that there, in the wilds of Canada, we had relied on a cell phone to locate ourselves on the map. And we had checked the phone every hour or two, because we needed to know where we were before we could figure out where we were going. If we could not find ourselves on the map, the destination didn't matter. We would not be arriving there. Losing our way for awhile, or taking a few unplanned detours, wouldn't usually concern me. But given the wildfires, this time it did. I didn't want to wander too far off course.

And that became a challenge the next day. We paddled out of a small lake, and through a narrow passage that opened on to an immense expanse of water which we had to cross. A fierce headwind and rolling whitecaps conjured storms I'd seen on Lake Michigan. It was the roughest water I could remember on any of our trips. So I wondered if we should try crossing or wait. Paul and Rob calmly discussed how to do it—by paddling directly into the waves, which I'd done before, but never in water that rough.

Off Rob and Paul went, paddling like mad into the whipping wind and rolling whitecaps, the bow dropping into each trough, and then bouncing up on the next crest. They had just enough strength and rhythm to move the boat slowly forward and in the right direction.

Then Kendall and I set out into the torrent, following our older brothers, like we always did. But after 100 yards of success, the wind hammered us sideways—parallel to the waves. We had a few seconds to turn the boat or be swamped and lose all our gear. We turned it, thankfully, and made our way back to shore. Rob and Paul paddled back, and we all spent the afternoon on the shore—fishing and waiting and hoping that the water would calm.

By late afternoon, it had improved some, but was still rough. Paul and Rob wanted to keep moving. "It's calmer now," they said. "And what if it's worse tomorrow? We could be windbound here for days." It was a couple of miles across, would be dark in two hours, and we didn't know where the portage was, or even which inlet we were aiming for. "Or it could clear tomorrow and be an easy paddle," I said. We went round and round for awhile, but Paul and Rob finally agreed that trying to cross and find a campsite in the dark was not a good idea. So we set up our tents, made dinner, and got out the Scotch.

An hour later we got into an argument. Everyone was tired, disappointed, and unsure due to the weather. Paul and Rob didn't seem completely convinced that we should have stopped rather than pushing on. This was not the first time we'd argued. No one in our family, including our parents, was a stranger to conflict. It was often how things got worked out. On other trips we had argued about cribbage rules and fishing strategies and who drank more than their nightly allotment of Scotch. But we also waded into deeper topics—politics and religion. We tend to agree on politics, but not always on religion. And that was the subject of our blow-out that night. As preacher's kids, who grew up in the church, we'd all developed our own views—ranging from disbelief to devout belief and everything in between. That's not what mattered in this argument though, or in the others. It's that each of us was always certain that we were the one who was *right*. Back and forth we went. At one point, I tried to yell over all of my brothers, arguing that no one was listening. Not effective.

The weather the next day was pristine: clear skies and a tailwind that blew us across the open water. The clouds of misunderstanding from the previous night also gradually broke up and cleared, as we paddled and told stories.

"Do you remember the bear that night on Bachawan Lake?"

"Do you remember that monster northern that pulled us through Pickerel Narrows?"

"What about that time I snapped my fishing pole getting that laker in?"

"Didn't *you* fall in too?"

"Yep. And it was in May. Colder than shit."

"Remember how worried Dad used to get?"

"Yeah, he always wanted to go back early."

"But he always had a great time."

"Yeah. It was like he was a kid again."

It was the balm of memory that always knit our frayed egos and tired bodies back together again, so we were once more *at home* with each other. No matter what happened on those trips, or in our lives, that was where we always ended up.

As we crossed the lake we paused for a few casts at an inviting rocky drop-off, and then stopped to check out a pictograph that Rob had noticed. At the entrance to the river, I looked up to see a bald eagle kiting on a thermal, rising into a bright blue moment of sky and wind. As I watched him soar higher, I wondered what *he* saw: four more of those loud, furless animals that sometimes drifted by. Maybe he was checking for a stringer of fish trailing behind the canoes.

We weren't pushing, but with the tailwind, before we knew it, we were only a few miles from the take-out bridge, where Kendall's truck was parked. So when we couldn't find a good campsite, we decided to just keep going and get a room at The White Otter in Atikokan that night (and a shower!).

When we reached the bridge, we pulled the canoes out and scrambled up the steep bank to the truck. We tied one canoe on, and then Ken and Rob drove the truck back to get the other car at the put-in site. In the meantime, Paul and I lugged all the gear up to the road. When Rob and Ken returned an hour later, we loaded the cars, and tied on the second canoe. Then we headed into town, to find something to eat and toss our trash—including the tattered maps. We didn't need them anymore, nor GPS, nor a compass. We could find our way home by heart.

Travel That Takes You Home

We are all bound by a covenant of reciprocity: plant breath for animal breath, winter and summer, predator and prey, grass and fire, night and day, living and dying. Water knows this, clouds know this. Soil and rocks know they are dancing in a continuous giveaway of making, unmaking, and making the earth again.
—Robin Wall Kimmerer, BRAIDING SWEETGRASS

A gauzy drape of clouds hung over the mountains like an old, familiar question. *What am I doing here?* The clouds looked thin and light, yet concealed the rocky, jagged beauty beyond. As I shifted to low gear, to climb the steep, winding road, the clouds slowly blew over, and the Western Cascades reappeared.

I was on my way to visit the H.J. Andrews Experimental Forest, in central Oregon, as part of a program that encouraged a creative dialogue between artists/writers and scientists. The hope is that the writers' searching for words in the woods will somehow converge with the scientists' researching for data. The language of metaphor against the language of measurement. The artist frames the image of a rotting hemlock log with words, to capture the continuity of life and death. The scientist captures the decaying log with numeric info: the rate of carbon emission in kilograms per year. Both kinds of perception matter: words and numbers, myth and math. But what's remarkable about this program—"The Long Term Ecological Reflection Project"—is how long-term it is: 200 years. From 2003 until 2203 hundreds of writers will visit "the Andrews" to enter an ongoing conversation with trees and trout and rocks—and scientists—about our evolving relationships in our shared home.[20]

First, the Andrews Forest in numbers: 15,000 acres of wilderness, 53 species of mammals, 164 species of birds, 3100 invertebrate species, 20 species of reptiles and amphibians, 505 plant species, seven feet of rainfall per year, a maximum elevation of 5340 feet, 40% of the forest is old growth, 25% was harvested for timber, the tallest tree is 299 feet high, the oldest about 700 years. Lookout Creek's mean annual discharge: 121.83 cubic feet per second.

The Andrews, which was established in 1948, is remote but not untouched. Hundreds of red, black, and white ribbons knotted around hemlock and fir and cedar branches mark various botanical studies. And dozens of thermometers and gauges and infra-red cameras monitor everything from tree surface temperature to leaf breakdown in streams, to how soil nutrients impact carbon storage, root decomposition, and nitrogen fixation in trees and other plants.

But back to my original question: The emphasis is on "I." What was *I* doing there? After ten hours of travel—four in a plane and six in a car—and still a half hour away from the Andrews, I was beginning to have doubts. Oregon is a gorgeous *drive-to* state, but I know little of the culture or ecology of the region. I'm a life-long Midwesterner—from Iowa, a *drive-through* state, which is economically productive, but with a damaged, defeated landscape.

I learned long ago what Iowa stands for: Idiot Out Walking Around. Who doesn't love such comic humility? I do. And maybe it's necessary. Iowa is not known for its national parks or forests, but for rivers and streams that are badly polluted by farm run-off. The highest "mountain" is Hawkeye Point, near Sibley, at 1,670 feet. The only ocean is green: 13 million acres of rippling, waving corn.

But even so, Iowa's beauty still inspires me whenever I visit: the sweet, musty scent of freshly cut hay, a raccoon waddling out of the weeds like a little furry tank, a few cattle grazing in a meadow at dusk in the soft, golden light. Or a boxful of cucumbers, sitting on a makeshift table along some gravel road, with a "help yourself," sign taped on. I lived in that ordinary, everyday beauty for twenty-five years, but didn't always appreciate it, nor how *at home* I felt there.

So how do we learn to see, and nurture, the beauty in nature—and to belong to it—wherever we are?

That's a question I hoped to explore during my stay at the Andrews. Beauty isn't hard to find there. Lichen-draped

Douglas-firs—600-years-old and 280 feet tall—formed a canopy over a complex understory that included hazelnut, vine maple, rhododendron, and dogwood. All of which filtered the cold, clear, trout-filled streams that tumbled through the woods. Decades of intensive study of the forest has yielded all kinds of useful insights to ecologists. One is that the old-growth canopy may buffer the wider ecosystem from rising temperatures caused by global warming. This moderation within the forest may also help conserve bird, amphibian, and insect populations, and other species that are temperature sensitive. And it might counteract the misaligned phenology caused by climate change: like if the temp-sensitive huckleberries fruit a month early (March), but a bird, whose migration is tied to light/day-length, still arrives in April to feast on the berries, and there are none left.

Though it is a site of intense research, the Andrews still felt like wilderness to me. Even the managed fir plantations—planted 60 years ago as a lumber crop—were as old as some of the woodlands I grew up with in Iowa, where everything is harvested. I remember an Iowa ad campaign motto in the seventies when I was a kid—"Iowa: A Place to Grow." The goal was to attract more tourists and residents. The problem was everyone knew they'd left out the final word: corn.

Iowa again. I'm not sure why the comparisons linger. I guess I had a chip on my shoulder. My Midwestern pride and identity is easily threatened. Though I didn't have Oregon-envy. I knew that the people were just as nutty and beautiful there as anywhere else. So what was it? I guess I worried about how much I could *see* in a Northwestern forest through the lens of a Midwestern life. I knew coyotes and cardinals and white pines, not newts and dippers and western hemlocks. What could I possibly write about? The same old fear: I was just a tourist.

Tourists only see what they come to see. They are collectors of bucket list destinations, to which they fly for a day or two in order to Snapchat a dozen selfies to prove they've arrived. "Here I am at Yellowstone." "Here we are at Glacier." The pictures all look the same. And since I've often been a tourist, I know how we think: short term. Which is why the "packaged tour" is so popular; it's contained and comfortable, yet exciting, and provides the immediate gratification we have come to expect. Yet such trips rarely allow us to get to know the natural wonders we so long to document on our cell phones.

But the searching/seeing at the Andrews Forest was long-term, and reflective, which was what interested me, as both ideas are antithetical to modern life. What does *long-term* mean in a frenetic culture of convenience, where Amazon will overnight a still-writhing Maine lobster or a pair of new running shoes to your front door in a few hours? Why *reflect*—a slow ponderous process—when the world demands that you *react*, that you Snap or Tweet?

Like an old-growth forest, true reflection takes time; it's slow and gradual. And like old-growth, it's increasingly rare.

In part because our sense of time has been radically altered. We are multi-present multi-taskers, who live in virtual realities, rather than in one real place at one time. The new hi-tech human animal is more productive, but less patient and attentive. That's why those flat, corn-fed Midwestern states, like Iowa, are no longer 5-hour drive-throughs, but 15-minute *fly-overs*. You don't even need to look anymore.

But some still do. I do. And I still long to spend most of my time on the ground, to be rooted somewhere. My hope: the difference between a drive-through state and a drive-to state, is not geographic spectacle—not snow-capped mountains or rocky coastlines—but within the driver, and what they're capable of seeing, and where they think they're going, and how they understand arrival. Any state is a drive-to state if you're paying attention. Which is the central point of the program at the Andrews Forest: to pay attention.

I climbed into my car to drive to the first Reflection Site—the Log Decomposition Plot, or "the Cathedral of Rot." My favorite term in the site description was "butt rot." It was pleasingly crass amid all of the scientific jargon. The butt/base of an old-growth tree could be rotting for a century before the tree fell and died. But it doesn't die. It decays. *Decay* means "to fall away"—to return to your constituent parts, what you're made of.

I creeped through the woods on a muddy one-lane national forest road, trying not to get stuck. The site was five miles from the Andrews headquarters. There was no cell reception and I didn't bring the two-way "emergency" radio they gave me—too heavy to carry. My rental car—a Mistubishi Mirage—was the kind that could be picked up and carried away by four large men. It didn't inspire confidence. Nor did warnings in my orientation packet to beware of cougars—particularly at dusk. Cougars are sighted from time to time, and they make frequent appearances on the four "game-cams"—which are mounted throughout the forest.

But no one I'd met had actually seen one at the Andrews. (Allow me to note here that a dozen cougars have been seen in boring old Iowa in recent years—the last one treed by dogs in a soybean field.) So the only vulnerability I felt was due to the physical isolation. Other people were as rare as cougars. If you got hurt out in the bush, it might take a ranger awhile to find you.

When I saw the cutout along the forest road, marking the trail to the Log Decomp Plot, I parked the car. As I tramped into the rainy forest an old question drifted up like the mist rising from the forest floor: *What am I doing here?* The forest felt foreign again—more tropical, more like Nicaragua or the Philippines, than Iowa. The Andrews is described as a quasi-Mediterranean climate—mild, moist winters and warm, dry summers. What I noticed was the furry drapes of moss hanging from the trees, and that it was raining "cabbage": grey-green pieces of crinkled, thick-veined leaves falling everywhere from the canopy 200 feet above. Lobaria, a lichen which only grows in forests 100+ years old, loosely attaches itself to branches and is easily blown to the ground. It fixes nitrogen directly from the air making it available for other plant and animal life, including on the forest floor, where mycorrhizal fungi transfer the nitrogen to host plants.

Mark Harmon, the forest ecologist who initiated the log decomp study, was also focused on ground decay. In 1985, working with the US Forest Service and other scientists, Harmon (the "head rotter"), cut down and sectioned four species of trees, each representing a different decay rate: silver fir (fastest decay), western hemlock, Douglas-fir, and western red cedar (slowest decay). He then dispersed the 500+ logs in six different old-growth locations in the Andrews—to monitor the rate/process of decay and its impact on the ecology of the forest. He is measuring everything from annual carbon emission to how the various decomposers (white rot fungi versus brown rot fungi) break down different parts (bark, heartwood, etc.) of the different tree species. Why does this matter, a non-scientist like me might ask. Because, according to Harmon, these different fungal groups and the varied rates of log decomposition impact nutrient cycling and carbon sequestration. Translation: his research shows that deadwood in native forests plays an essential role in carbon storage and in maintaining the forest's ecological balance.

After a ten-minute hike I arrived at the log decomp site: a scattering of 12-foot-long log sections lying about in various states of decay. Some were sawn into cross-sections, or "cookies," for analyzing nitrogen and "rot zones" and the impact of invertebrates. A large diameter PVC pipe was glued to the flank of a red cedar log to sample its CO_2 output. The red cedar's bark and heartwood were hard and firm. This tree would take 500 years or more to completely break down, exceeding the length of the study, which is also 200 years (ending in 2185). The silver fir log next to the cedar, however, had nearly disappeared since the study began, two-thirds of the tree rotting back into the earth and blowing off into the atmosphere. I stuck my finger into the damp mush of the heartwood. After just 35 or 40 years this tree will have disintegrated, rotting into rich new soil in which seeds can take root.

That day, sitting there amid the rotting logs, the idea of *time* felt oddly relative, and elusive. So did death. Consider the work of fungal mycelia. And of the bark beetles, who open pathways for other decomposers with their chaotic galleries. I looked at one in a silver fir log for a long time. This evolving maze of decay, where life and death seem to converge, felt like a work of art.

One discovery Mark Harmon made is that a decaying log can contain more living tissue than a live tree. "The tree that's green and standing up is the one they should call 'dead,'" he says. "The tree down on the ground is the one that's really alive." A dead tree is more alive than a live one. Death is not an endmark—a period—but an ellipsis. The living process of decay is both a *break* between life and death and a *bridge*.

I often think of this break/bridge, and about *how* we are alive (or not), when I read the work of Oregon poet, William Stafford. The day I arrived at the Andrews Forest I copied his poem "*Quo Vadis*" on a note card and taped it over my writing desk—the same poem I taped over my desk in my office, back home, more than thirty years ago. The poem is a question that I still live in. *Where are you going?*

Quo Vadis

Sometimes I choose a cloud and let it
cross the sky floating me away.
Or a bird unravels its song and carries me
as it flies deeper and deeper into the woods.

Is there a way to be gone and still
belong? Travel that takes you home?

Is that life?—to stand by a river and go.

To stand by a river and go. The image lingered the next morning, as I stepped out into the rain and headed toward the second long-term reflection site: the gravel bar on Lookout Creek.

Rain drip-ticked on the yellow maple leaves above me. Drop-tocked in the puddles collecting on the ground. Ping-ticked on the shiny black cedar log. Plop-tocked on the overturned plastic bucket some researcher left. Though the wet drum of rain was nuanced and lovely, when I got within 100 yards of the creek, the rush of whitewater overwhelmed everything.

Travel that takes you home. If I was only on my way *to* somewhere, like a tourist, I might end up in a state I didn't want to visit—the state of longing—rather than Stafford's "home" state of *belonging*, where I still hoped to arrive.

I sat on a flat rock in the hard rain listening to Lookout Creek. Given the downpour, and all the rocks and deadfalls, it had a lot to say. Over time, the gurgling water dissolves rock, rots logs and leaves and carries them downstream, along with trout and pine pollen and needles and cones, and bits of moss and lichen. Over time it will reshape its bed and banks and habitat, physically describing its character and history in the forest. Over time, its diversity and biological health will be denigrated due to climate change and other human activities. Over time, as with all streams and rivers, it will measure and reveal both our culpability and response-ability as a species. Over time it will measure who we are.

Over time. Not *in* or *on* time. Not hours or numbers, but a river of light and darkness, of heat and cold. Over time, things change. Some change is dramatic—what ecologists call "a disturbance"—like the rotting 400-year-old Douglas-fir that fell across the creek 40 years ago. The crashing tree ripped a wide gash in the canopy, prompting slower, less dramatic change below: a thick stand of alder trees sprung up from the gravel bar amid the flood of new light. When the Doug-fir fell, its bole and branches obstructed and partly dammed the creek, forming a deep pool—where, over time, native trout came to live, and to wait and watch for midges to light on the water.

Waiting and watching. Over time. To stand by a river and go. That rainy day I lingered by the water all afternoon, scrambling around on the slippery rocks like the child I once was—completely lost in the moment—and hoping to see someone: a bird, a snake, a beetle, a frog, or anyone who lived there.

Just before leaving, when I looked down into the deep blue pool behind the fallen Doug-fir, a cutthroat trout appeared—maybe eight inches long, his spotted back a foot below the surface—slowly drifting, scanning for bugs. Could he see me? As I watched him, I couldn't help but think of the red-tailed hawks I love. And how they too hang and drift, but in a softer, deeper blue—over an Iowa hayfield, waiting and watching for a mouse to wander out of the grass into the open sunlight, where death awaits. And life.

Death and life. Walking along the gushing creek back to my room, I pondered their continuity—life into death, death into life—and their convergence. I wondered about that bottomless moment when the rushing water finally reached the ocean, and suddenly, yet completely, became a part of the whole. The movement slowing to a deepening stillness.

Travel that takes you home.

Words of Thanks

The first person to thank is also my first reader—Carol. Her patient support and editing insights are always essential to my work. She, and our adult children—Tessa, Abby, and Bennett—still create *home* for me, a place where we all belong. And thanks, also, for their graciously allowing me to sometimes include snippets from their lives in my writing.

Thanks to Ice Cube Press, and its founder/director, Steven Semken, for his support, insights, and careful eye for detail in the design and editing of this book. I can't imagine a better home for this work.

Thanks to Andrew Fate for his creative expertise in designing the cover and to artist Marcia Wegman for letting us use her lovely pastel painting, *Newport Road in February*.

Thanks to Francis and Suzanne White Lance on the Pine Ridge Reservation, and to Lita Calilan, Luna and Perla Dingayan, and Digna and Juancho Compañano in the Philippines. These patient cross-cultural mentors welcomed Carol and me into their communities with a rare kindness and hospitality.

Thanks to the following writer and teacher friends, for their generosity and editorial assistance: Phil Andres, Mike Branch, Cindy and Jeff Crosby, Kirk Daddow, Todd Davis, Hope Edelman, Tim Fate, Roberta Gates, Jeanne and Chuck Jorgensen, Cassie Kircher, Stina Kielsmeier-Cook, Carl Klaus, Patrick Madden, Bob Majerus, David McGrath, Michael Mc-

Gregor, Harley McIlrath, Michele Morano, Angela Morales, Marc Nieson, Bob Root, Scott Russell Sanders, Susan Sink, Mary Swander, Dave Wilson, and Lauren Winner.

Thanks to my dear friend, John Price, for his insights and support. His feedback was invaluable.

Thanks to Rev. Bill Lovin, my parents' pastor in Iowa City, for his kindness and wisdom.

Thanks to cin salach and Chris Green, for including me in the Tiger Room Reading Series, which allowed me to try out some of these essays on a live audience.

Thanks to Michael McDermott and my colleagues at the Black Earth Institute, for their support and inspiration.

Thanks to the following institutions and people, who helped create the time and space needed to complete this book: The Collegeville Institute in Collegeville, MN for a semester-long residency and fellowship (Carla Durand, Vivian Krueger, Don Ottenhoff); the College of Dupage (Glen Ellyn, IL) for a year-long sabbatical; The AgArts Foundation (Mary Swander, Carolyn Levine) for a two-week residency at the White Rock Conservancy (Elizabeth Garst) in Coon Rapids, Iowa; and The Spring Creek Project at Oregon State University (Fred Swanson) for a two-week residency at the H.J. Andrews Forest (Blue River, OR).

And finally, thanks to my comrades at the Covenant Farm in Sawyer, Michigan, where I often go to write. Their friendship and support, and those 70 acres of forest and meadow, always inspire my work.

Notes

1 William Stafford, "Quo Vadis" from *The Way It Is: New and Selected Poems.* Copyright © 1998 by William Stafford and the Estate of William Stafford. Reprinted with the permission of The Permissions Company, LLC, on behalf of Graywolf Press, Minneapolis, Minnesota, graywolfpress.org.

2 Thoreau, Henry David. *Walden; or Life in the Woods.* Boston: Ticknor and Fields, 1854.

3 Sanders, Scott Russell. *Writing from the Center.* Bloomington: Indiana UP, 1995.

4 Fahmy, Dalia. "Key Findings About Americans' Belief in God." The Pew Research Center, 2018. https://www.pewresearch.org/fact-tank/2018/04/25/key-findings-about-americans-belief-in-god/

5 Forche, Carolyn. *The Angel of History.* Harper: New York, 1995.

6 Postman, Neil. *Technopoly: The Surrender of Culture to Technology.* Vintage: N.Y., 1993.

7 Hirschfield, Jane. *Ten Windows: How Great Poems Transform the World.* Knopf: N.Y., 2015.

8 Merton, Thomas. *A Search for Solitude: Pursuing the Monk's True Life. The Journals of Thomas Merton* (Vol. 3: 1952-1960) New York: Harper One, 1997.

9 Kenyon, Jane. "Let Evening Come." *Otherwise: New and Selected Poems.* Graywolf Press: St. Paul, 1996.

10 Twenge, Jeanne. *iGen:Why Today's Super-Connected Kids Are Growing Up Less Rebellious, More Tolerant, Less Happy—and Completely Unprepared for Adulthood—and What That Means for the Rest of Us.* Atria Books: New York, 2017.

11 This term was coined by conservative journalist Georgie Ann Geyer because so many Americans visiting Nicaragua were wearing Birkenstocks. It was meant to highlight our naivete.

12 Renato Constantino, *The Philippines: A Past Revisited*, vol.1, Quezon City, Philippines: Renato Constantino, 1975.

13 This is an Hebraic analogy that my Old Testament professor in seminary liked to use. The origins are unclear.

14 The family records show that his military service was cut short due to chronic dysentery, so he was sent home on a Hospital Ship, arriving back in San Francisco Sept. 8, 1899.

15 Rosaldo, Renato. *Truth and Culture: The Remaking of Social Analysis*. Beacon: Boston, 1993.

16 According to the 2020 census, Allen is one of the poorest communities in the United States. The household median income is $12,000.00 and 83% of the 450 residents live below the poverty line.

17 These stats come from several sources: US Census, 2020; re-member.org; "Traveling Pine Ridge Today," *South Dakota Magazine*, 2019.

18 Shortly after this piece was written, the State of Nebraska voted to close the liquor stores in White Clay. So residents of the Pine Ridge Reservation instead make alcohol runs to other nearby Nebraska towns. And vodka is now the drink of choice, not beer, as it is easily diluted, and sold for elevated prices.

19 See "The Battle for the Black Hills," by Nick Estes. *High Country News*: Jan, 2021.

20 The long-term ecological reflection program described here is "The Spring Creek Project for Ideas, Nature, and the Written Word," and is a collaboration of Oregon State University, the Andrews Forest, and the National Forest Service.

Photo credits*

p. 20 Maquoketa River and dam (photo by Sherri Oswalt)

p. 22 Bennett Fate, Quetico Provincial Park, Ontario, CA

p. 52 Stella Maris Chapel window, Collegeville, Minnesota

p. 55 Stella Maris Chapel, Collegeville, Minnesota

p. 66 Delores Fate (hands)

p. 67 Delores Fate swimming (photo by Robin Fate)

p. 85 Dolores and Johanna (Nicaragua)

p. 90 Sandinista rally in Chinandega (Nicaragua)

p. 94 Plantain vendor and child (Nicaragua)

p. 99 Market in Laoag (Philippines)

p. 112 US soldiers with Gatling Gun (Manila, 1899). Library
of Congress/Getty Images

p. 120 "The Six Grandfathers": Mount Rushmore before
carving (1919)

p. 126 Road signs near Pine Ridge, South Dakota

p. 132 Sweat lodge near Allen, South Dakota

p. 151 H.J. Andrews Research Forest, near Blue River, Oregon

p. 156 Beetle gallery, H.J. Andrews Research Forest

p. 158 Lookout Creek, H.J. Andrews Research Forest

*All photos were taken by the author, except where noted.

The Ice Cube Press began publishing in 1991 to focus on how to live with the natural world and to better understand how people can best live together in the communities they share and inhabit. Using the literary arts to explore life and experiences in the heartland of the United States we have been recognized by a number of well-known writers including: Bill Bradley, Gary Snyder, Gene Logsdon, Wes Jackson, Patricia Hampl, Greg Brown, Jim Harrison, Annie Dillard, Ken Burns, Roz Chast, Jane Hamilton, Daniel Menaker, Kathleen Norris, Janisse Ray, Craig Lesley, Alison Deming, Harriet Lerner, Richard Lynn Stegner, Richard Rhodes, Michael Pollan, David Abram, David Orr, and Barry Lopez. We've published a number of well-known authors including: Mary Swander, Jim Heynen, Mary Pipher, Bill Holm, Connie Mutel, John T. Price, Carol Bly, Marvin Bell, Debra Marquart, Ted Kooser, Stephanie Mills, Bill McKibben, Craig Lesley, Elizabeth McCracken, Derrick Jensen, Dean Bakopoulos, Rick Bass, Linda Hogan, Pam Houston, Paul Gruchow and Bill Moyers. Check out Ice Cube Press books on our web site, join our email list, Facebook group, or follow us on Twitter. Visit booksellers, museum shops, or any place you can find good books and support our truly honest to goodness independent publishing projects and discover why we continue striving to "hear the other side."

Ice Cube Press, LLC (Est. 1991)
North Liberty, Iowa, Midwest, USA

Resting above the Silurian and Jordan aquifers
steve@icecubepress.com Check us out on twitter and facebook
www.icecubepress.com

Celebrating Thirty Years of Independent Publishing

To Fenna Marie—
coming or going
staying or leaving
you're my home in motion.